The Seventeenth Century
Bacon Through Marvell

GOLDENTREE BIBLIOGRAPHIES
In Language and Literature
under the series editorship of
O. B. Hardison, Jr.

The Seventeenth Century: Bacon Through Marvell

compiled by

Arthur E. Barker

The University of Western Ontario

AHM Publishing Corporation
Arlington Heights, Illinois 60004

ISBN 0-88295-548-9, paper
ISBN 0-88295-570-5, cloth

Library of Congress Card Number: 76-4657

PRINTED IN THE UNITED STATES OF AMERICA

Contents

CONTENTS

Preface

THIS BIBLIOGRAPHY is intended for graduate and advanced undergraduate students in courses about the poetry and prose of the seventeenth century in England. It does not include the drama, which is covered by another volume in this series. Shakespeare and Milton are also covered in separate volumes. Some figures who are transitional are included in one of three other Goldentree Bibliographies: *The Sixteenth Century: Skelton Through Hooker*; *The Age of Dryden*; or *The Eighteenth Century*. The selection in this volume covers the literature into 1975, illustrates the varying approaches and developing preoccupations of the past forty years, represents the wide variety of critical approaches and scholarly concerns of the past dozen or so years, and includes some accounts of the continental context and significant reappraisals of the reputation and influence of seventeenth-century authors. A few very minor authors have been excluded, although the specializing student will find them covered by items in the section, Aids to Research. Although the selection includes many brief explicatory items, especially significant older comments and recent interpretations of important poems, the specialist should consult the files of such periodicals as *Notes and Queries, Explicator,* and *Seventeenth-Century News* for other items. The selection does not include unpublished M.A. and Ph.D. dissertations, which are listed in *Dissertation Abstracts* and *Dissertation Abstracts International*. It includes some authoritative general studies in languages other than English, but it does not record specialized articles in other languages.

The aim of this bibliography is to assist the student in surveying a topic, writing reports and term papers, preparing for examinations, and doing independent reading. The compiler has therefore attempted to steer a middle course between the brief lists of references included in the textbooks and guides and the long professional bibliography in which significant items are lost in the sheer number of references given. For major authors, where the representation of interests requires a relatively large number of items, the listings have been subdivided into comprehensive studies and studies of particular topics or works.

The coincidence of the later stages in the preparation of this publication with a change of status to a part-time, postretirement appointment invited the recalling of many indebtednesses, accumulated over forty years. The selection depends much on contributions made by undergraduate and graduate students and research assistants in half a dozen Canadian and American universities. Including the names of so many of these in the following pages has induced much reminiscence and satisfaction. Special acknowledgment must be made of the assistance of the D. B. Weldon Library of the University of Western Ontario and particularly of its Collections Librarian: English, Ms. Linda Dowler, and of the otherwise unacknowledged help of Dorothy Barker in, among other ways, searching, checking, and proofing.

Attention is called to the following features of the bibliography:

1. Extra margin on each page permits listing of library call numbers of often-used items.

2. Extra space at the bottom of each page permits inclusion of additional entries.

3. An index by author follows the bibliography proper.

4. All items are numbered consecutively throughout the book. Thus each title can be readily identified by its own number, both in the cross reference and in the Index.

In a small number of cases, a change in the numbering system of this bibliography has resulted in the elimination of a number. There are no entries for numbers 146, 207, 534, 566, 708, 1890, and 1958.

Journals are abbreviated in the standard forms given in the Table of Symbols at the beginning of recent PMLA bibliographies. A list of abbreviations frequently cited follows this preface.

Abbreviations

Ariel	Ariel: A Quarterly Review of the Arts and Sciences in Israel
ArielE	Ariel: A Review of International English Literature
ATR	Anglican Theological Review
AUMLA	Journal of the Australasian Universities Language and Literature Association
BJRL	Bulletin of the John Rylands Library
BRMMLA	Bulletin of the Rocky Mountain Modern Language Association
BSUF	Ball State University Forum
BuR	Bucknell Review
BUSE	Boston University Studies in English
CCC	College Composition and Communication
CE	College English
CEA	CEA Critic
CentR	Centennial Review
CH	Church History
CL	Comparative Literature
CLAJ	College Language Association Journal
ClioW	Clio: An Interdisciplinary Journal of Literature, History and the Philosophy of History: Wisconsin
CLS	Comparative Literature Studies
CompD	Comparative Drama
CP	Concerning Poetry
CR	Critical Review
CritQ	Critical Quarterly
CSR	Christian Scholar's Review
Daedalus	Daedalus: Proceedings of the American Academy of Arts and Sciences
DUJ	Durham University Journal
E&S	Essays and Studies by Members of the English Association
EA	Etudes Anglaises
EIC	Essays in Criticism
ELH	Journal of English Literary History
ELN	English Language Notes
ELR	English Literary Renaissance
EM	English Miscellany
EN	English Notes

EngR	English Record
EnlE	Enlightenment Essays
ES	English Studies
ESA	English Studies in Africa
Expl	Explicator
ForumH	Forum (Houston)
GorR	Gordon Review
Greyfriar	Greyfriar: Siena Studies in Literature
HAB	Humanities Association Bulletin (Canada)
HINL	History of Ideas Newsletter
HLB	Harvard Library Bulletin
HLQ	Huntington Library Quarterly
HSL	Hartford Studies in Literature
HTR	Harvard Theological Review
HudRev	Hudson Review
JAAC	Journal of Aesthetics and Art Criticism
JEGP	Journal of English and Germanic Philology
JHI	Journal of the History of Ideas
JMRS	Journal of Medieval and Renaissance Studies
JRUL	Journal of the Rutgers University Library
JSP	Journal of Social Psychology
JWCI	Journal of the Warburg and Courtauld Institutes
KR	Kenyon Review
L&P	Literature and Psychology
Lang&L	Language and Literature
Lang&S	Language and Style
LHR	Lock Haven Review
LM	Literature Moderne
LURev	Lakehead University Review
M&H	Medievalia et Humanistica
MLN	Modern Language Notes
MLQ	Modern Language Quarterly
MLR	Modern Language Review
ModA	Modern Age
Mosaic	Mosaic: A Journal for the Study of Comparative Literature and Ideas
MP	Modern Philology
MR	Massachusetts Review
N&Q	Notes and Queries
NDQ	North Dakota Quarterly
Neophil	Neophilologus
NLH	New Literary History
NM	Neuphilologische Mitteilungen
NS	Die Neueren Sprachen
OR	Oxford Review
OUR	Ohio University Review
PAPS	Proceedings of the American Philosophical Society
PBA	Proceedings of the British Academy
PBSA	Papers of the Bibliographical Society of America
PCP	Pacific Coast Philology
Person	Personalist

ABBREVIATIONS

PLL	Papers on Language and Literature
PMASAL	Papers of the Michigan Academy of Science, Arts and Letters
PMLA	Publications of the Modern Language Association of America
PQ	Philological Quarterly
PS	Pacific Spectator
PULC	Princeton University Library Chronicle
QJS	Quarterly Journal of Speech
Ren	Renascence
RenP	Renaissance Papers
RenQ	Renaissance Quarterly
RES	Review of English Studies
RLMC	Rivista di Letterature Moderne e Comparate
RLV	Revue des Langues Vivantes
RMS	Renaissance and Modern Studies
RN	Renaissance News
RomN	Romance Notes
RPol	Review of Politics
SAQ	South Atlantic Quarterly
SB	Studies in Bibliography
SCB	South Central Bulletin
SCN	Seventeenth-Century News
SEL	Studies in English Literature, 1500 – 1900
SLitI	Studies in the Literary Imagination
SM	Speech Monographs
SN	Studia Neophilologica
SNL	Satire Newsletter
SoR	Southern Review
SoRA	Southern Review: An Australian Journal of Literary Studies
SP	Studies in Philology
SR	Sewanee Review
SRen	Studies in the Renaissance
SSL	Studies in Scottish Literature
TC	Twentieth Century
Theoria	Theoria: A Journal of Studies in the Arts, Humanities and Social Sciences
TSE	Tulane Studies in English
TSL	Tennessee Studies in Literature
TSLL	Texas Studies in Literature and Language
UCSLL	University of Colorado Studies in Language and Literature
UMSE	University of Mississippi Studies in English
UR	University Review
UTQ	University of Toronto Quarterly
UTSH	University of Tennessee Studies in Humanities
UWR	University of Windsor Review
VQR	Virginia Quarterly Review
WHR	Western Humanities Review
XUS	Xavier University Studies
YES	Yearbook of English Studies

Note: *The publisher and compiler invite suggestions for additions to future editions of the bibliography.*

Aids to Research:
Bibliographies, Guides, Surveys

1 ALLISON, A. F., ed. *Four Metaphysical Poets. Pall Mall Bibliographies*, 3. London: Dawson, 1973.

2 BARKER, A. E., et al. "Recent Studies in the English Renaissance." *SEL*, no. 1, annually, 1961 –.

3 BENNETT, H. S. *English Books and Readers, III: 1603–1640*. London: Cambridge University Press, 1970.

4 BERRY, L. E., ed. *A Bibliography of Studies in Metaphysical Poetry, 1939–1960*. Madison: University of Wisconsin Press, 1964.

5 BUSH, D., ed. "Bibliography." See **78**.

6 DYSON, A. E., ed. *English Poetry: Select Bibliographical Guides*. New York: Oxford University Press, 1971.

7 FORD, B., ed. *A Guide to English Literature, Vol. 3: From Donne to Marvell*. Baltimore: Penguin, 1956.

8 FRANK, J., ed. *Hobbled Pegasus: A Descriptive Bibliography of Minor English Poetry, 1641–1660*. Albuquerque: University of New Mexico Press, 1968.

9 HARLOW, G., et al., eds. *The Year's Work in English Studies*. London: Oxford University Press; London: Murray; New York: Humanities Press; annually, 1921 –.

10 HORDEN, J., and J. B. MISENHEIMER, Jr., eds. *Annual Bibliography of English Language and Literature*. Modern Humanities Research Association, annually, 1920 –.

11 MESEROLE, H. T., et al., eds. *MLA Bibliography* and *International Bibliography*. Supplement to *PMLA*, annually, 1922 –.

12 PATRICK, J. M., and H. T. MESEROLE, eds. *Seventeenth-Century News*. University Park: Pennsylvania State University 1950 –.

13 PINTO, V. de S. *The English Renaissance, 1510–1688*. London: Cresset, 1951.

14 POLLARD, A. W., et al., eds. *Short-Title Catalogue of Books Printed in England, Scotland and Ireland . . . , 1475–1640*. London: Bibliographical Society, 1926, 1963, etc.

15 "Recent Studies in Renaissance Authors: [Annotated Bibliographies]." *ELR*, 1 (1971), etc.

16 RUOFF, J. E. *Crowell's Handbook of Elizabethan and Stuart Literature*. New York: Crowell, 1975.

17 SPENCER, T., and M. VAN DOREN, eds. *Studies in Metaphysical Poetry: Two Essays and a Bibliography*. New York: Columbia University Press, 1939; Port Washington: Kennikat, 1964.

18 TANNENBAUM, S. A., and D. R. TANNEBAUM, eds. *Elizabethan Bibliographies*. Port Washington: Kennikat, 1967.

1

19 WATSON, G., et al., eds. *The New Cambridge Bibliography of English Literature.* London: Cambridge University Press, 1969—.

20 WELLS, W., et al., eds. "Recent Literature of the English Renaissance, 1600—1660." *SP,* annually, 1922—.

21 WING, D. G., ed. *Short-Title Catalogue of Books Printed in England, Scotland, Ireland . . . , 1641—1700.* New York: Index Society, 1945—51; Vol. I, second edition, revised and enlarged, New York: Index Committee, Modern Language Association, 1972.

Anthologies

22 BALD, R. C., ed. *Seventeenth-Century English Poetry.* New York: Harper & Row, 1959.

23 BRINKLEY, R. F., ed. *English Prose of the Seventeenth Century.* New York: Norton, 1951.

24 BROADBENT, J. B., ed. *Classic Poets of the Seventeenth Century.* Bergenfield: New American Library, 1974.

25 CUTTS, J. P., ed. *Seventeenth Century Songs and Lyrics: Collected and Edited from the Original Music Manuscripts.* Columbia: University of Missouri Press, 1959.

26 CUTTS, J. P., and F. KERMODE, eds. *Seventeenth-Century Songs.* Reading: University School of Art, 1956.

27 DALGLISH, J., ed. *Eight Metaphysical Poets.* New York: Macmillan, 1961.

28 DAVID, B., and E. DAVIS, eds. *Poets of the Early Seventeenth Century.* London: Routledge & Kegan Paul, 1967.

29 FELLOWES, E. H., ed. *English Madrigal Verse, 1588—1632.* Third edition, revised and enlarged by F. W. Sternfeld and D. Greer. New York: Oxford University Press, 1967.

30 FERRY, A. D., ed. *Seventeenth-Century English Minor Poets.* New York: Dell, 1964.

31 FERRY, A. D., ed. *Religious Prose of Seventeenth-Century England.* New York: Knopf, 1967.

32 GARDNER, H., ed. *The Metaphysical Poets.* Baltimore: Penguin, 1957; New York, Oxford University Press, 1961; second edition, revised, 1967.

33 GILBERT, A. H., ed. *Literary Criticism: Plato to Dryden.* New York: American Book Co., 1940; Detroit. Wayne State University Press, 1962.

34 GRENNEN, J., ed. *The Poetry of John Donne and the Metaphysical Poets.* New York: Monarch, 1965.

35 GRIERSON, H. J. C., ed. *Metaphysical Lyrics and Poems of the Seventeenth Century.* New York: Oxford University Press, 1921, 1959.

36 HARDISON, O. B., Jr., ed. *English Literary Criticism: The Renaissance.* New York: Appleton-Century-Crofts; Englewood Cliffs: Prentice-Hall, 1963.

ANTHOLOGIES

37 HARRIS, V., and I. HUSAIN, eds. *English Prose, 1600—1660.* New York: Holt, Rinehart, and Winston, 1965.

38 HARRISON, T. P., and H. J. LEON, eds. *The Pastoral Elegy.* Austin: University of Texas Press, 1959.

39 HEBEL, J. W., and H. H. HUDSON, eds. *Poetry of the English Renaissance.* New York: Appleton-Century-Crofts; Englewood Cliffs: Prentice-Hall, 1929.

40 HEBEL, J. W., et al., eds. *Prose of the English Renaissance.* New York: Appleton-Century-Crofts, 1952.

41 HONIG, E., and O. WILLIAMS, eds. *The Major Metaphysical Poets of the Seventeenth Century.* New York: Washington Square, 1968.

42 HUSSEY, M., ed. *Jonson and the Cavaliers.* London: Heinemann, 1964; New York: Barnes & Noble, 1966.

43 KENNER, H., ed. *Seventeenth-Century Poetry: The Schools of Donne and Jonson.* New York: Holt, Rinehart, and Winston, 1964.

44 KERMODE, F., ed. *English Pastoral Poetry from the Beginnings to Marvell.* London: Harrap, 1952.

45 LEVER, J. W. *Sonnets of the English Renaissance.* London: University of London, 1974.

46 LEWALSKI, B. K., and A. J. SABOL, eds. *Major Poets of the Earlier Seventeenth Century.* New York: Odyssey, 1973.

47 MACLEAN, H. N., ed. *Ben Jonson and The Cavalier Poets.* New York: Norton, 1974.

48 MAHL, M. R., ed. *Seventeenth-Century English Prose.* New York: Lippincott, 1968.

49 MARTZ, L. L., and R. S. SYLVESTER, eds. *English Seventeenth-Century Verse,* 2 vols. Garden City: Doubleday, 1969; New York: Norton, 1973.

50 MISH, C. C., ed. *Short Fiction of the Seventeenth Century.* Garden City: Doubleday; New York: New York University Press, 1963.

51 NOVARR, D., ed. *Seventeenth-Century English Prose.* New York: Knopf, 1967.

52 PARTRIDGE, A. C., ed. *The Tribe of Ben: Pre-Augustan Classical Verse in English.* London: Arnold, 1966.

53 PINTO, V. de S., ed. *English Biography in the Seventeenth Century: Selected Short Lives.* London: Harrap, 1951.

54 PRIEST, H. M., ed. *Renaissance and Baroque Lyrics: An Anthology of Translations from the Italian, French, and Spanish.* Evanston: Northwestern University Press, 1962.

55 SEGAL, H. *The Baroque Poem: A Comparative Survey.* New York: Dutton, 1974.

56 SHAABER, M. A., ed. *Seventeenth-Century English Prose.* New York: Harper, 1967.

57 SHAWCROSS, J. T., and R. D. EMMA, eds. *Seventeenth-Century English Poetry.* New York: Lippincott, 1969.

58 SMITH, G. G., ed. *Elizabethan Critical Essays.* Oxford: Clarendon Press, 1904.

59 SPINGARN, J. E., ed. *Critical Essays of the Seventeenth Century.* Oxford: Clarendon Press, 1908–9; Bloomington: Indiana University Press, 1957.

60 STARKMAN, M. K., ed. *Seventeenth-Century English Poetry,* 2 vols. New York: Knopf, 1967.

61 TAYLER, E. W., ed. *Literary Criticism of Seventeenth-Century England.* New York: Knopf, 1967.

62 URE, P., ed. *Seventeenth-Century Prose.* Baltimore: Penguin, 1956.

63 VICKERS, B, ed. *Seventeenth-Century Prose.* Harlow: Longmans, 1969.

64 WARNKE, F. J., ed. *European Metaphysical Poetry.* New Haven: Yale University Press, 1961.

65 WHITE, H. C., R. C. WALLERSTEIN, and R. QUINTANA, eds. *Seventeenth-Century Verse and Prose.* New York: Macmillan, 1951–52; Vol. I, revised edition, 1971.

66 WILLY, M., ed. *The Metaphysical Poets.* London: Arnold, 1971.

67 WITHERSPOON, A. M., and F. J. WARNKE, eds. *Seventeenth-Century Prose and Poetry.* New York: Harcourt, Brace & World, 1963; second edition, 1969.

Literary History and Criticism

General

68 ALLEN, D. C., ed. *Studies in Honor of T. W. Baldwin,* Urbana: University of Illinois Press, 1958.

69 ALLEN, D. C. *Mysteriously Meant: The Rediscovery of Pagan Symbolism and Allegorical Interpretation in the Renaissance.* Baltimore: Johns Hopkins Press, 1970.

70 ATKINS, J. W. H. *English Literary Criticism: The Renaissance.* London: Methuen, 1947, 1951.

71 Atkins, J. W. H. *English Literary Criticism: Seventeenth and Eighteenth Centuries.* London: Methuen, 1951.

72 BABB, L. *The Elizabethan Malady: A Study of Melancholia in English Literature from 1580 to 1642.* East Lansing: Michigan State University Press, 1951.

73 BAKER, H. *The Dignity of Man: Studies in the Persistence of an Idea.* Cambridge: Harvard University Press, 1947. Reprinted as *The Image of Man.* New York: Harper, 1961.

74 BAKER, H. *The Wars of Truth: Studies in the Decay of Christian Humanism in the Earlier Seventeenth Century.* Cambridge: Harvard University Press, 1952.

75 BARKER, A. E. "The Earlier Seventeenth Century." *JEGP*, 62 (1963), 617–28.

76 BETHELL, S. L. *The Cultural Revolution of the Seventeenth Century.* London: Dobson, 1951.

77 BRINKLEY, R. F., ed. *Coleridge on the Seventeenth Century.* Durham: Duke University Press, 1955.

78 BUSH, D. *English Literature in the Earlier Seventeenth Century, 1600–1660.* Oxford: Clarendon Press, 1945; revised edition, 1962.

79 COLIE, R. L. *Paradoxia Epidemica: The Renaissance Tradition of Paradox.* Princeton: Princeton University Press, 1966.

80 CRAIG, H. *The Enchanted Glass: The Elizabethan Mind in Literature.* New York: Oxford University Press, 1936; Oxford: Blackwell, 1962.

81 DANIELLS, R. "Baroque Form in English Literature." *UTQ*, 14 (1944–45), 393–408.

82 DANIELLS, R. "English Baroque and Deliberate Obscurity." *JAAC*, 5 (1947), 115–21.

83 DANIELLS, R. "The Mannerist Element in English Literature." *UTQ*, 36 (1966–67), 1–11.

84 DAVIS, H., and H. GARDNER, eds. *Elizabethan and Jacobean Studies Presented to Frank Percy Wilson.* Oxford: Clarendon Press, 1959.

85 DAY, M. S. *History of English Literature;* Vol. I, *To 1660.* Garden City: Doubleday, 1963.

86 ELIOT, T. S. *Selected Essays.* London: Faber and Faber; New York: Harcourt, Brace, 1932, 1951, etc.

87 FISCH, H. *Jerusalem and Albion: The Hebraic Factor in Seventeenth-Century Literature.* New York: Schocken, 1964.

88 FISH, S. E. *Self-Consuming Artifacts: The Experience of Seventeenth-Century Literature.* Berkeley: University of California Press, 1972.

89 FREEMAN, R. *English Emblem Books.* London: Chatto & Windus, 1948; New York: Octagon Books, 1966.

90 GRIERSON, H. J. C. *Cross-Currents in English Literature of the Seventeenth Century.* London: Chatto & Windus, 1929, 1958; New York: Harper Torchbooks, 1958; Baltimore: Penguin, 1966.

91 HALL, V. *Renaissance Literary Criticism.* New York: Columbia University Press, 1945; Gloucester: Peter Smith, 1959.

92 HAMILTON, K. G. *The Two Harmonies: Poetry and Prose in the Seventeenth Century.* Oxford: Clarendon Press, 1963.

93 HANSEN, N.B. *That Pleasant Place: The Representation of Ideal Landscape in English Literature from the Fourteenth to the Seventeenth Century.* Copenhagen: Akademisk Forlag, 1973.

94 HARDIN, R. F. "Ovid in Seventeenth-Century England." *CL*, 24 (1972), 44–62.

95 HARDISON, O. B., Jr. *The Enduring Monument: A Study of the Idea of Praise in Renaissance Literary Theory and Practice.* Chapel Hill: University of North Carolina Press, 1962; New York: Greenwood, 1973.

96 HARRIS, V. *All Coherence Gone: A Study of the Seventeenth-Century Controversy Over Disorder and Decay in the Universe.* Chicago: University of Chicago Press, 1949; London: Cass, 1966.

97 HAYDN, H. C. *The Counter-Renaissance.* New York: Scribner's, 1950; New York: Grove Press, 1960.

98 HIGHET, G. *The Classical Tradition: Greek and Roman Influences on Western Literature.* New York: Oxford University Press, 1949.

99 HOLDEN, W. P. *Anti-Puritan Satire, 1572–1642.* New Haven: Yale University Press, 1954.

100 HOOPES, R. *Right Reason in the English Renaissance.* Cambridge: Harvard University Press, 1962.

101 JONES, R. F., et al. *The Seventeenth Century: Studies in the History of English Thought and Literature from Bacon to Pope.* Stanford: Stanford University Press, 1951, 1965.

102 KERMODE, F. "Dissociation of Sensibility." *KR*, 19 (1957), 169–94.

103 KING, J. R. *Studies in Seventeenth-Century Writers.* Athens: Ohio University Press, 1966.

104 KNIGHTS, L. C. *Explorations: Essays in Criticism Mainly on the Literature of the Seventeenth Century.* London: Chatto & Windus, 1946; Stanford: Stanford University Press, 1966.

105 LEWIS, C. S. *English Literature in the Sixteenth Century.* Oxford: Clarendon Press, 1954.

106 LYONS, B. G. *Voices of Melancholy: Studies in Literary Treatments of Melancholy in Renaissance England.* New York: Norton, 1975.

107 MACKLEM, M. *The Anatomy of the World: Relations Between Natural and Moral Law from Donne to Pope.* Minneapolis: University of Minnesota Press, 1958.

108 MALLOCH, A. E. "The Techniques and Function of the Renaissance Paradox." *SP*, 53 (1956), 191–203.

109 MAZZEO, J. A., ed. *Reason and the Imagination: Studies in the History of Ideas, 1600–1800.* New York: Columbia University Press, 1962.

110 MAZZEO, J. A. *Renaissance and Seventeenth-Century Studies.* New York: Columbia University Press, 1964.

111 MAZZEO, J. A. *Renaissance and Revolution: Backgrounds to Seventeenth-Century English Literature.* New York: Random House, 1965.

112 McCANLES, M. *Dialectical Criticism and Renaissance Literature.* Berkeley: University of California Press, 1975.

113 MILBURN, D. J. *The Age of Wit, 1650–1750.* New York: Macmillan, 1966.

114 MINER, E., ed. *Seventeenth-Century Imagery: Essays on Uses of Figurative Language from Donne to Farquhar.* Berkeley: University of California Press, 1971.

115 MULDER, J. R. *The Temple of the Mind: Education and Literary Taste in Seventeenth-Century England.* New York: Western Publishing, 1969.

116 NICOLSON, M. H. *Science and Imagination.* Ithaca: Cornell University Press, 1956.

117 NICOLSON, M. H. *Mountain Gloom and Mountain Glory: The Development of the Aesthetics of the Infinite.* Ithaca: Cornell University Press, 1959.

118 OSMOND, R. "Body and Soul Dialogues in the Seventeenth Century." *ELR,* 4 (1974), 364–403.

119 RICKS, C., ed. *English Poetry and Prose, 1540–1674.* London: Barrie & Jenkins, 1970.

120 ROSSKY, W. "Imagination in the English Renaissance: Psychology and Poetic." *SRen,* 5 (1958), 49–73.

121 SANDBANK, S. "On the Structure of Some Seventeenth-Century Metaphors." *ES,* 52 (1971), 323–30.

122 SASEK, L. A. *The Literary Temper of the English Puritans.* Baton Rouge: Louisiana State University Press, 1961.

123 *Seventeenth-Century Studies Presented to Sir Herbert Grierson.* Oxford: Clarendon Press, 1938; New York: Octagon, 1967.

124 SLOAN, T. O. "Rhetoric and Meditation: Three Case Studies." *JMRS,* 1 (1971), 45–58.

125 SOUTHALL, R. *Literature and the Rise of Capitalism.* London: Lawrence and Wishart, 1973.

126 SPINGARN, J. E. *A History of Literary Criticism in the Renaissance.* New York: Columbia University Press, 1899, 1924.

127 SPITZER, L. *Classical and Christian Ideas of World Harmony.* Baltimore: Johns Hopkins Press, 1963.

128 SYPHER, W. *Four Stages of Renaissance Style: Transformations in Art and Literature, 1400–1700.* Garden City: Doubleday, 1955.

129 TAYLER, E. W. *Nature and Art in Renaissance Literature.* New York: Columbia University Press, 1964.

130 WARNKE, F. J. *Versions of Baroque: European Literature in the Seventeenth Century.* New Haven: Yale University Press, 1972.

131 WEBBER, J. "Stylistics: A Bridging of Life and Art in Seventeenth-Century Studies." *NLH,* 2 (1971), 283–96.

132 WEDGWOOD, C. V. *Seventeenth-Century English Literature.* New York: Oxford University Press, 1950.

133 WEIDHORN, M. *Dreams in Seventeenth-Century Literature.* The Hague: Mouton, 1970.

134 WILEY, M. L. *The Subtle Knot: Creative Scepticism in Seventeenth-Century England.* London: George Allen & Unwin, 1952; New York: Greenwood, 1968.

135 WILEY, M. L. *Creative Sceptics.* New York: Hillary House, 1967.

136 WILLEY, B. *The Seventeenth-Century Background: Studies in the Thought of the Age in Relation to Poetry and Religion.* London: Chatto & Windus, 1934; New York: Columbia University Press, 1952; Garden City: Doubleday, 1953; Harmondsworth: Penguin, 1972.

137 WILLIAMS, R. *The Country and the City.* New York: Oxford University Press, 1973.

138 WILLIAMSON, G. *Seventeenth-Century Contexts.* Chicago: University of Chicago Press, 1961.

139 WILLIAMSON, G. *Milton and Others.* Chicago: University of Chicago Press, 1965.

140 WILSON, E. C. *Prince Henry and English Literature.* Ithaca: Cornell University Press, 1946.

141 WILSON, F. P. *Elizabethan and Jacobean.* Oxford: Clarendon Press, 1946.

Poetry

142 ALLEN, D. C. *Image and Meaning: Metaphoric Traditions in Renaissance Poetry.* Baltimore: Johns Hopkins Press, 1960; revised edition, 1968.

143 ALVAREZ, A. *The School of Donne.* London: Chatto & Windus; New York: Random House, 1961.

144 BAKER, C. D. "Certain Religious Elements in the English Doctrine of the Inspired Poet During the Renaissance." *ELH,* 6 (1939), 300–323.

145 BARKER, A. E. "An Apology for the Study of Renaissance Poetry." *Literary Views,* ed. C. Camden. Chicago: Chicago University Press, 1964.

147 BEER, P. *An Introduction to the Metaphysical Poets.* Totowa: Rowman & Littlefield, 1972.

148 BENNETT, J. *Five Metaphysical Poets: Donne, Herbert, Vaughan, Crashaw, Marvell.* Cambridge: Cambridge University Press, 1964.

149 BETHELL, S. L. "The Nature of Metaphysical Wit." *Northern Miscellany of Literary Criticism,* 1 (1953), 19–40; and see **958.**

150 BINNS, J. W., ed. *The Latin Poetry of English Poets.* Boston: Routledge & Kegan Paul, 1974.

151 BRADNER, L. *Musae Anglicanae: A History of Anglo-Latin Poetry, 1500–1925.* New York: Modern Language Association; London: Oxford University Press, 1940.

152 BREDVOLD, L. I. "The Rise of English Classicism: Study in Methodology." *CL,* 2 (1950), 253–68.

153 BROADBENT, J. B. *Poetic Love.* London: Chatto & Windus, 1964; New York: Barnes & Noble, 1965.

154 BROWN, J. R., and B. HARRIS, eds. *Metaphysical Poetry.* Stratford-upon-Avon Studies, 11. London: Arnold, 1970.

155 BUSH, D. *Mythology and the Renaissance Tradition in English Poetry.* Minneapolis: University of Minnesota Press, 1932; revised edition, New York: Norton, 1963.

156 CLARK, D. L. *Rhetoric and Poetry in the Renaissance: A Study of Rhetorical Terms in English Renaissance Literary Criticism.* New York: Columbia University Press, 1922; New York: Russell & Russell, 1963.

157 COHEN, J. M. *The Baroque Lyric.* London: Hutchinson; New York: Hillary House, 1963.

158 COLIE, R. L. *The Resources of Kind: Genre-Theory in the Renaissance.* Berkeley: University of California Press, 1973.

159 COLLMER, R. G. "The Meditation on Death and its Appearance in Metaphysical Poetry." *Neophil*, 45 (1961), 323—33.

160 CRUTTWELL, P. *The Shakespearean Moment and its Place in the Poetry of the Seventeenth Century.* London: Chatto & Windus, 1954; and see **47**.

161 CUNNINGHAM, J. V. *Tradition and Poetic Structure: Essays in Literary History and Criticism.* Denver: Swallow, 1960.

162 DE MOURGUES, O. *Metaphysical, Baroque, and Précieux Poetry.* Oxford: Clarendon Press, 1953.

163 DE MOURGUES, O. "The European Background to Baroque Sensibility." See **7**.

164 DOUGHTY, W. L. *Studies in Religious Poetry of the Seventeenth Century.* London: Epworth Press, 1946; Port Washington: Kennikat, 1969.

165 DUNCAN, J. E. *The Revival of Metaphysical Poetry . . . , 1800 to the Present.* Minneapolis: University of Minnesota Press, 1959.

166 DUNDAS, J. "Levity and Grace: The Poetry of Sacred Wit." *YES*, 2 (1972), 93—102.

167 EDWARDS, T. R. *Imagination and Power: A Study of Poetry on Public Themes.* London: Chatto & Windus, 1971.

168 ELIOT, T. S. "The Metaphysical Poets." See **86** and **878**.

169 ELLRODT, R. *L'inspiration personelle et l'esprit du temps chez les poétes métaphysique anglais,* 3 vols. Paris: Corti, 1960.

170 ELLRODT, R. "Scientific Curiosity and Metaphysical Poetry in the Seventeenth Century." *MP*, 61 (1964), 180—97.

171 EMPSON, W. *Seven Types of Ambiguity.* London: Chatto & Windus, 1930; revised edition, 1947; Baltimore: Penguin, 1961.

172 EMPSON, W. *Some Versions of Pastoral: [English Pastoral Poetry].* London: Chatto & Windus, 1935; Norfolk: New Directions, 1950.

173 ESCH, A. "Structure and Style in some Minor Religious Epics of the Seventeenth Century." *Anglia*, 78 (1960), 40—54.

174 FARLEY-HILLS, D. *The Benevolence of Laughter: Comic Poetry of the Commonwealth and Restoration.* New York: Rowman & Littlefield, 1975.

175 FINNEY, G. L. *Musical Backgrounds for English Literature, 1580—1650.* New Brunswick: Rutgers University Press, 1962.

176 FISHER, W. N. "*Occupatio* in Sixteenth- and Seventeenth-Century Verse." *TSLL*, 14 (1972), 203—22.

177 GOLDBERG, J. "Hesper-Vesper: Aspects of Venus in a Seventeenth-Century Trope." *SEL*, 15 (1975), 37—55.

178 GRANT, P. *The Transformation of Sin: Studies in Donne, Herbert, Vaughan and Traherne.* Montreal: McGill-Queen's University Press; Amherst: University of Massachusetts Press, 1974.

179 GRUNDY, J. *The Spenserian Poets: A Study in Elizabethan and Jacobean Poetry.* London: Arnold, 1969.

180 HALEWOOD W. H. *The Poetry of Grace: Reformation Themes and Structure in Seventeenth-Century Poetry.* New Haven: Yale University Press, 1970.

181 HAMMOND, G., ed. *The Metaphysical Poets: A Casebook*. London: Macmillan, 1974.

182 HARRISON, J. S. *Platonism in English Poetry of the Sixteenth and Seventeenth Centuries*. New York: Columbia University Press, 1903.

183 HENINGER, S. K., Jr. "Metaphor as Cosmic Correspondence." *Medieval and Renaissance Studies*, ed. J. M. Hedley, Chapel Hill: University of North Carolina Press, 1968.

184 HENINGER, S. K., Jr. *Touches of Sweet Harmony: Pythagorean Cosmology and Renaissance Poetics*. San Marino: Huntington Library, 1974.

185 HIBBARD, G. R. "The Country House Poem of the Seventeenth Century." *JWCI*, 19 (1956), 159−74. *Essential Articles for the Study of Alexander Pope*, ed. M. Mack. Hamden: Shoe String, 1964.

186 HINMAN, R. B. "The Apotheosis of Faust: Poetry and the New Philosophy in the Seventeenth Century." *Stratford-upon-Avon Studies*, 11 (1970), 149−80.

187 HOLLANDER, J. *The Untuning of the Sky: Ideas of Music in English Poetry, 1500−1700*. Princeton: Princeton University Press, 1961.

188 HUGHES, R. E. "Metaphysical Poetry as Event." *HSL*, 3 (1971), 191−96.

189 HUNTER, J. *The Metaphysical Poets*. London: Evans, 1965.

190 HUSAIN, I. *The Mystical Element in the Metaphysical Poets of the Seventeenth Century*. Edinburgh: Oliver and Boyd, 1948; New York: Biblo and Tannen, 1966.

191 HUTTON, J. "Some English Poems in Praise of Music." *EM*, 2 (1951), 1−64.

192 JOHNSON, P. *Form and Transformation in Music and Poetry of the English Renaissance*. New Haven: Yale University Press, 1972.

193 JOHNSON, S. *Lives of the English Poets [1779−1781]*, ed. G. B. Hill. Oxford: Clarendon Press, 1905; New York: Octagon, 1967, ed. A. Waugh; New York: Oxford University Press, 1906, etc.

194 JONAS, L. *The Divine Science: The Aesthetics of Some Representative Seventeenth-Century English Poets*. New York: Columbia University Press, 1940; New York: Octagon, 1973.

195 KEAST, W. R. "Johnson's Criticism of the Metaphysical Poets." *ELH*, 17 (1950), 59−70.

196 KEAST, W. R., ed. *Seventeenth-Century English Poetry: Modern Essays in Criticism*. New York: Oxford University Press, 1962; second edition, 1971.

197 KERMODE, F., ed. *The Metaphysical Poets: Key Essays . . . .* Greenwich: Fawcett, 1969.

198 KORSHIN, P. J. "The Evolution of Neoclassic Poetics: Cleveland, Denham, and Waller as Poetic Theorists." *Eighteenth-Century Studies*, 2 (1968), 102−37.

199 LEAVIS, F. R. *Revaluation: Tradition and Development in English Poetry*. London: Chatto & Windus, 1936; New York: Norton, 1963; Baltimore: Penguin, 1964.

200 LeCOMTE, E. S. *Poets' Riddles: Essays in Seventeenth-Century Explications*. Port Washington: Kennikat, 1974.

201 LEISHMAN, J. B. *The Metaphysical Poets: Donne, Herbert, Vaughan, Traherne.* Oxford: Clarendon Press, 1934; New York: Russell & Russell, 1963.

202 LEVINE, J. A. "The Status of the Verse Epistle Before Pope." *JEGP,* 59 (1960), 658—84.

203 MADDISON, C. *Apollo and the Nine: A History of the Ode.* Baltimore: Johns Hopkins Press, 1960.

204 MAHOOD, M. M. *Poetry and Humanism.* New Haven: Yale University Press, 1950; New York: Norton, 1970.

205 MALLOCH, A. E. "The Unified Sensibility and Metaphysical Poetry." *CE,* 15 (1953), 95—101.

206 MARTZ, L. L. *The Poetry of Meditation: A Study in English Religious Literature of the Seventeenth Century.* New Haven: Yale University Press, 1954; revised edition, 1962.

208 MARTZ, L. L. *The Paradise Within: Studies in Vaughan, Traherne, and Milton.* New Haven: Yale University Press, 1964.

209 MARTZ, L. L. *The Wit of Love: Donne, Carew, Crashaw, Marvell.* Notre Dame: University of Notre Dame Press, 1969.

210 MARTZ, L. L. *The Poem of the Mind: Essays on Poetry, English and American.* New York: Oxford University Press, 1966.

211 MAZZEO, J. A. "A Critique of Some Modern Theories of Metaphysical Poetry." *MP,* 50 (1952), 88—96; and see **878** and **958.**

212 McEUEN, K. A. *Classical Influence Upon the Tribe of Ben.* Cedar Rapids: Torch, 1939.

213 MILES, J. "The Primary Language of Poetry in the 1640's." *University of California Publications in English,* 19 (1948), 1—160.

214 MILLER, P. W. "The Decline of the English Epithalamion." *TSLL,* 12 (1970), 405—16.

215 MINER, E. *The Metaphysical Mode from Donne to Cowley.* Princeton: Princeton University Press, 1969.

216 MINER, E. *The Cavalier Mode from Jonson to Cotton.* Princeton: Princeton University Press, 1971; and see **47.**

217 MOLESWORTH, C. "Property and Virtue: The Genre of the Country-House Poem in the Seventeenth Century." *Genre,* 1 (1968), 141—57.

218 MORRIS, B. "Satire from Donne to Marvell." *Stratford-upon-Avon Studies,* 11 (1970), 211—36.

219 NELSON, L., Jr. *Baroque Lyric Poetry.* New Haven: Yale University Press, 1961.

220 NEVO, R. *The Dial of Virtue: A Study of Poems on Affairs of State in the Seventeenth Century.* Princeton: Princeton University Press, 1963.

221 NICOLSON, M. H. *The Breaking of the Circle: Studies in the Effect of the "New Science" upon Seventeenth-Century Poetry.* Evanston: Northwestern University Press, 1950; revised edition, New York: Columbia University Press, 1960.

222 PALMER, D. J. "The Verse Epistle." *Stratford-upon-Avon Studies,* 11 (1970), 73—100.

11

223 PARTRIDGE, A. C. *The Language of Renaissance Poetry*. London: Deutsch, 1971.

224 PERKINS, D. D. "Johnson on Wit and Metaphysical Poetry." *ELH*, 20 (1953), 200–217.

225 PETERSON, D. *The English Lyric from Wyatt to Donne: A History of the Plain and Eloquent Styles*. Princeton: Princeton University Press, 1967.

226 PHILLIPS, J. E. "Poetry and Music in the Seventeenth Century." *Stuart and Georgian Moments*, ed. E. Miner. Berkeley: University of California Press, 1972.

227 POULET, G. *The Metamorphoses of the Circle*, trans. G. Dawson and E. Coleman. Baltimore: Johns Hopkins Press, 1966.

228 PRAZ, M. *The Flaming Heart*. Garden City: Doubleday, 1958.

229 PRAZ, M. *Studies in Seventeenth-Century Imagery*. Rome: Edizioni di Storia e Letteratura, 1939–47; second edition, enlarged, 1964.

230 RAY, D. E. "Seventeenth-Century Poetry and Science: Twin Champions Against Ignorance." *Proceedings: Pacific Northwest Conference on Foreign Languages*. Victoria: University of Victoria, 1970.

231 RICHMOND, H. M. *The School of Love: The Evolution of the Stuart Love Lyric*. Princeton: Princeton University Press, 1964.

232 RIVERS, I. *The Poetry of Conservatism, 1600–1745: A Study of Poets and Public Affairs from Jonson to Pope*. Cambridge: Rivers Press, 1973.

233 ROSS, M. M. *Poetry and Dogma: The Transfiguration of Eucharistic Symbols in Seventeenth-Century Poetry*. New Brunswick: Rutgers University Press, 1954; New York: Octagon, 1969.

234 SAUNDERS, J. W. "The Social Situation of Seventeenth-Century Poetry." *Stratford-upon-Avon Studies*, 11 (1970), 237–60.

235 SCOULAR, K. W. *Natural Magic: Studies in the Presentation of Nature in English Poetry from Spenser to Marvell*. Oxford: Clarendon Press, 1965.

236 SEWELL, E. *The Orphic Voice: Poetry and Natural History*. New Haven: Yale University Press, 1960.

237 SHAFER, R. *The English Ode to 1660*. Princeton: Princeton University Press, 1918.

238 SHARP, R. L. *From Donne to Dryden: The Revolt against Metaphysical Poetry*. Chapel Hill: University of North Carolina Press, 1940.

239 SHUSTER, G. N. *The English Ode from Milton to Keats*. New York: Columbia University Press, 1940.

240 SKELTON, R. *The Cavalier Poets*. London, New York: Longmans, Green, 1960; New York: Oxford University Press, 1970.

241 SLOAN, T. O., and R. B. WADDINGTON, eds. *The Rhetoric of Renaissance Poetry*. Berkeley: University of California Press, 1974.

242 SMITH, A. J. "The Metaphysic of Love." *RES*, 9 (1958), 362–75.

243 SMITH, A. J. "The Failure of Love: Love Lyrics after Donne." *Stratford-upon-Avon Studies*, 11 (1970), 41–72.

244 SPENCER, J. B. *Heroic Nature: Ideal Landscape in English Poetry from Marvell to Thomson*. Evanston: Northwestern University Press, 1973.

245 STEWART, S. *The Enclosed Garden: Tradition and Image in Seventeenth-Century Poetry*. Madison: University of Wisconsin Press, 1966.

246 SUMMERS, J. H. *The Heirs of Donne and Jonson*. New York: Oxford University Press, 1970; and see **47**.

247 SWARSDON, H. R. *Poetry and the Fountain of Light: Observations on the Conflict between Christian and Classical Traditions in Seventeenth-Century Poetry*. Columbia: University of Missouri Press, 1962.

248 SWEDENBERG, H. T. *The Theory of the Epic in England, 1650–1850*. Berkeley: University of California Press, 1944.

249 TUVE, R. *Elizabethan and Metaphysical Imagery: Renaissance Poetic and Twentieth-Century Critics*. Chicago: University of Chicago Press, 1947.

250 VARMA, R. S. *Imagery and Thought in the Metaphysical Poets: With Special Reference to Andrew Marvell*. Mystic: Verry, 1972.

251 VICKERS, B. *Classical Rhetoric in English Poetry*. London: Macmillan, 1970.

252 WALLACE, J. M. "Examples are Best Precepts: Readers and Meanings in Seventeenth-Century Poetry." *Critical Inquiry*, 1 (1974), 273–90.

253 WALLERSTEIN, R. C. "The Development of the Rhetoric and Metre of the Heroic Couplet, Especially in 1625–1645." *PMLA*, 50 (1935), 166–209.

254 WALLERSTEIN, R. C. *Studies in Seventeenth-Century Poetic*. Madison: University of Wisconsin Press, 1950.

255 WALTON, G. *Metaphysical to Augustan; Studies in Tone and Sensibility in the Seventeenth Century*. London: Bowes & Bowes, 1955.

256 WALTON, G. "The Cavalier Poets." See **7**.

257 WARNKE, F. J. "Sacred Play: Baroque Poetic Style." *JAAC*, 22 (1964), 455–64.

258 WARNKE, F. J. "Metaphysical Poetry and the European Context." *Stratford-upon-Avon Studies*, 11 (1970), 261–76.

259 WATSON, G. "The Language of the Metaphysicals." *Literary English Since Shakespeare*, ed. G. Watson. London: Oxford University Press, 1970.

260 WEDGWOOD, C. V. *Poetry and Politics under the Stuarts*. Cambridge: Cambridge University Press, 1960.

261 WHIPPLE, T. K. *Martial and the English Epigram from Sir Thomas Wyatt to Ben Jonson*. New York: Phaeton, 1970.

262 WHITE, H. C. *The Metaphysical Poets; A Study in Religious Experience*. New York: Macmillan, 1936; New York: Collier, 1962.

263 WILLIAMSON, G. *The Donne Tradition: A Study in English Poetry from Donne to the Death of Cowley*. Cambridge: Harvard University Press, 1930; New York: Octagon, 1973.

264 WILLIAMSON, G. *The Proper Wit of Poetry*. Chicago: University of Chicago Press, 1961.

265 WILLIAMSON, G. *Six Metaphysical Poets: A Readers' Guide*. New York: Farrar, Straus, and Giroux, 1967.

266 WILLY, M. *Three Metaphysical Poets [Crashaw, Vaughan, Traherne]*. London, New York: Longmans, Green, 1961.

Prose

267 ADOLPH, R. *The Rise of Modern Prose Style.* Cambridge: Harvard University Press, 1968.

268 ALLEN, D. C. "Style and Certitude [from More to Bacon]." *ELH,* 15 (1948), 167 – 75.

269 BOTTRALL, M. *Every Man a Phoenix: Studies in Seventeenth-Century Autobiography.* London: Murray, 1958.

270 BOYCE, B. *The Theophrastan Character in English.* Cambridge: Harvard University Press, 1947; New York: Humanities Press, 1967.

271 CRANE, W. G. *Wit and Rhetoric in the Renaissance: The Formal Basis of Elizabethan Prose Style.* New York: Columbia University Press, 1937.

272 CROLL, M. W. *Style, Rhetoric and Rhythm: Essays,* ed. J. M. Patrick et al. Princeton: Princeton University Press, 1966.

273 DAVIS, W. R. *Idea and Act in Elizabethan Fiction.* Princeton: Princeton University Press, 1969.

274 DELANY, P. *British Autobiography in the Seventeenth Century.* New York: Columbia University Press, 1969.

275 EBNER, D. *Autobiography in Seventeenth-Century England: Theology and the Self.* The Hague: Mouton, 1971.

276 FISH, S., ed. *Seventeenth-Century Prose: Modern Essays in Criticism.* New York: Oxford University Press, 1971.

277 JONES, R. F. "The Rhetoric of Science in England of the Mid-Seventeenth Century." *Restoration and Eighteenth-Century Literature: Essays,* ed. C. Camden. Chicago: University of Chicago Press, 1963.

278 JONES, R. F. "Science and Language in England of the Mid-Seventeenth Century." See **101** and **276.**

279 JONES, R. F. "Science and English Prose Style in the Third Quarter of the Seventeenth Century." See **101** and **276.**

280 MATTHEWS, W. "Seventeenth-Century Autobiography." *Autobiography, Biography, and the Novel,* ed. W. Matthews and R. W. Rader. Los Angeles: Clark Memorial Library, 1973.

281 MAZZEO, J. A. "Seventeenth-Century English Prose Style: The Quest for a Natural Style." *Mosaic,* 6 (1973), 107 – 44.

282 MINER, E. "Inclusive and Exclusive Decoration in Seventeenth-Century Prose." *Lang & S,* 5 (1972), 192 – 203.

283 SMITH, D. I. B., ed. *Editing Seventeenth-Century Prose.* Toronto: Hakkert, 1972.

284 STAPLETON, L. *The Elected Circle: Studies in the Art of Prose.* Princeton: Princeton University Press, 1973.

285 STAUFFER, D. *English Biography before 1700.* Cambridge: Harvard University Press, 1930.

286 THOMPSON, E. N. S. *The Seventeenth-Century English Essay.* Iowa City: Iowa University Press, 1926; New York: Haskell House, 1967.

287 WEBBER, J. *The Eloquent "I": Style and Self in Seventeenth-Century Prose.* Madison: University of Wisconsin Press, 1968.

288 WILLIAMSON, G. *The Senecan Amble: A Study in Prose from Bacon to Collier.* Chicago: University of Chicago Press, 1951.

289 WILLIAMSON, G. "Senecan Style in the Seventeenth Century." See **139** and **276**.

290 WILSON, F. P. *Seventeenth-Century Prose.* Berkeley: University of California Press, 1960.

Backgrounds

Intellectual and Aesthetic

291 ALLEN, B. S. *Tides in English Taste (1619—1800): A Background for the Study of Literature.* Cambridge: Harvard University Press, 1937.

292 ALLEN, D.C. *The Star-Crossed Renaissance: The Quarrel About Astrology and Its Influence in England.* Durham: Duke University Press, 1941; New York: Octagon, 1966.

293 ALLEN, D. C. *Doubt's Boundless Sea: Skepticism and Faith in the Renaissance.* Baltimore: Johns Hopkins Press, 1964.

294 AUERBACH, E. *Mimesis: The Representation of Reality in Western Literature.* Princeton: Princeton University Press, 1953; Garden City: Doubleday, 1957.

295 AUERBACH, E. "Figura." *Scenes from the Drama of European Literature.* New York: Meridian, 1959.

296 BAMBOROUGH, J. B. *The Little World of Man.* New York: Longmans, Green, 1952.

297 BATTENHOUSE, R. W. "The Doctrine of Man in Calvin and in Renaissance Platonism." *JHI,* 9 (1948), 447—71.

298 CASSIRER, E. *The Platonic Renaissance in England,* trans. by J. P. Pettegrove. Austin: University of Texas Press, 1953.

299 COSTELLO, W. T. *The Scholastic Curriculum at Early Seventeenth-Century Cambridge.* Cambridge: Harvard University Press, 1958.

300 CURTIS, M. H. *Oxford and Cambridge in Transition, 1558—1642.* Oxford: Clarendon Press, 1959.

301 HAUSER, A. *Mannerism: The Crisis of the Renaissance and the Origin of Modern Art.* London: Routledge & Kegan Paul, 1965.

302 HOWELL, W. S. *Logic and Rhetoric in England, 1500—1700.* Princeton: Princeton University Press, 1956; New York: Russell & Russell, 1961.

303 Howes, R. F., ed. *Historical Studies of Rhetoric and Rhetoricians.* Ithaca: Cornell University Press, 1961.

15

BACKGROUNDS

304 HUNTER, W. B., Jr. "The Seventeenth-Century Doctrine of Plastic Nature." *HTR*, 43 (1950), 197–213.

305 LEEUVEN, H. G. Van. *The Problem of Certainty in English Thought, 1630–1690.* The Hague: Nijhoff, 1963.

306 LEVIN, H. *The Myth of the Golden Age in the Renaissance.* New York: Oxford University Press, 1969.

307 LOVEJOY, A. O. *The Great Chain of Being.* Cambridge: Harvard University Press, 1936, 1960.

308 MASON, D. E. *Music in Elizabethan England.* Washington, D.C.: Folger Shakespeare Library, 1958.

309 MILLER, P. *The New England Mind: The Seventeenth Century.* Cambridge: Harvard University Press, 1954.

310 OGDEN, H. V. S. "Variety and Contrast in Seventeenth-Century Aesthetics." *JHI*, 10 (1949), 159–82.

311 OGDEN, H. V. S. and M. S. *English Taste in Landscape in the Seventeenth Century.* Ann Arbor: University of Michigan Press, 1956.

312 ONG, W. J. "System, Space, and Intellect in Renaissance Symbolism." *Bibliothèque d'Humanisme et Renaissance,* 18 (1956), 222–39.

313 ONG, W. J. *Ramus, Method, and the Decay of Dialogue: From the Art of Discourse to the Art of Reason.* Cambridge: Harvard University Press, 1958.

314 PANOFSKY, E. *Meaning in the Visual Arts.* Garden City: Doubleday, 1955.

315 PANOFSKY, E. *Studies in Iconology: Humanistic Themes in the Art of the Renaissance.* New York: Harper & Row, 1962.

316 PANOFSKY, E. *Idea: A Concept in Art History.* Columbia: University of South Carolina Press, 1968.

317 PORTER, H. C. *Reformation and Reaction in Tudor Cambridge.* Cambridge: Cambridge University Press, 1958.

318 QUINONES, R. J. *The Renaissance Discovery of Time.* Cambridge: Harvard University Press, 1972.

319 QUINTANA, R. "Notes on English Educational Opinion during the Seventeenth Century." *SP*, 27 (1930), 265–92.

320 RØSTVIG, M.-S. *The Happy Man: Studies in the Metamorphoses of a Classical Ideal, 1600–1700.* Oxford: Blackwell, 1954; New York: Humanities Press, 1958.

321 SAUNDERS, J. L. *Justus Lipsius: The Philosophy of Renaissance Stoicism.* New York: Liberal Arts Press, 1955.

322 SELLS, L. *The Italian Influence on Englishmen in the Seventeenth Century.* Bloomington: Indiana University Press, 1964.

323 SENA, J. F. "Melancholic Madness and the Puritans." *HTR,* 66 (1973), 293–309.

324 SEZNEC, J. *The Survival of the Pagan Gods: The Mythological Tradition and its Place in Renaissance Humanism and Art.* New York: Pantheon, 1953; New York: Harper & Row, 1961.

325 SPROTT, S. E. *The English Debate on Suicide from Donne to Hume.* La Salle: Open Court, 1961.

BACKGROUNDS

326 STARNES, D. T., and E. W. TALBERT. *Classical Myth and Legend in Renaissance Dictionaries: A Study in Renaissance Dictionaries and their Relation to the Classical Learning of Contemporary English Writers.* Chapel Hill: University of North Carolina Press, 1955.

327 TILLYARD, E. M. W. *The Elizabethan World Picture: A Study of the Idea of Order in the Age of Shakespeare, Donne and Milton.* London: Chatto & Windus, 1943; New York: Random House, 1961; Baltimore: Penguin, 1963.

328 WARHAFT, S. "Stoicism, Ethics, and Learning in Seventeenth-Century England." *Mosaic,* 1, iv (1968), 82–94.

329 WEBSTER, C., ed. *The Intellectual Revolution of the Seventeenth Century.* London, Boston: Routledge & Kegan Paul, 1974.

330 WHIFFEN, M. *An Introduction to Elizabethan and Jacobean Architecture.* London: Art and Technics, 1952.

331 WIND, E. *Pagan Mysteries in the Renaissance.* New Haven: Yale University Press, 1958; enlarged, 1968; New York: Norton, 1968.

332 WINNY, J., ed. *The Frame of Order: An Outline of Elizabethan Belief Taken from Treatises of the Late Sixteenth Century.* New York: Barnes & Noble, 1957.

333 WOODFILL, W. L. *Musicians in English Society from Elizabeth to Charles I.* Princeton: Princeton University Press, 1953.

334 YATES, F. A. *Giordano Bruno and the Hermetic Tradition.* London: Routledge & Kegan Paul, 1964.

335 YATES, F. A. *The Art of Memory.* London: Routledge & Kegan Paul, 1966.

336 YATES, F. A. *Theatre of the World.* Chicago: University of Chicago Press, 1969.

Scientific

337 BOAS, M. *The Scientific Renaissance: 1450–1630.* New York: Harper, 1962.

338 BURLAND, C. A. *The Arts of the Alchemists.* New York: Macmillan, 1968.

339 BURTT, E. A. *The Metaphysical Foundations of Modern Physical Science.* London: K. Paul, Trench, Trubner; New York: Harcourt, Brace, 1925; revised editions, 1932, 1954.

340 BUSH, D. *Science and English Poetry: A Historical Sketch, 1590–1950.* New York: Oxford University Press, 1950.

341 BUTTERFIELD, H. *The Origins of Modern Science.* London: Bell, 1949; New York: Macmillan, 1956; New York: Free Press, 1965.

342 CROMBIE, A. C. *Augustine to Galileo,* or *Medieval and Early Modern Science.* London: Falcon, 1952; Garden City: Doubleday, 1959; Cambridge: Harvard University Press, 1961.

343 DAMPIER, W. *A History of Science and its Relations with Philosophy and Religion.* Cambridge: Cambridge University Press, 1929; revised edition, 1943.

17

BACKGROUNDS

344 DE ROLA, S. K. *The Secret Art of Alchemy.* London: Thames & Hudson, 1973.

345 HALL, A. R. *The Scientific Revolution 1500–1800; the Formation of the Modern Scientific Attitude.* London: Green, 1954.

346 HARRE, R., ed. *Early Seventeenth-Century Scientists.* London: Pergamon, 1966.

347 HENINGER, S. K. *A Handbook of Renaissance Meteorology.* Durham: Duke University Press, 1960.

348 HOENIGER, F. D. and J. F. M. *The Development of Natural History in Tudor England.* Washington, D.C.: Folger Shakespeare Library, 1969.

349 HOENIGER, F. D. and J. F. M. *The Growth of Natural History in Stuart England.* Washington, D.C.: FOLGER Shakespeare Library, 1969.

350 HOLMYARD, E. J. *Alchemy.* Baltimore: Penguin, 1957.

351 JOHNSON, F. R. *Astronomical Thought in Renaissance England: A Study of Scientific Writings from 1500 to 1645.* Baltimore: Johns Hopkins Press, 1937; New York: Octagon, 1968.

352 JONES, R. F. *Ancients and Moderns: A Study of the Rise of the Scientific Movement in Seventeenth-Century England.* St. Louis: Washington University, 1936; revised edition, 1961; Berkeley: University of California Press, 1965.

353 KOCHER, P. H. "Paracelsan Medicine in England: The First Thirty Years (ca. 1570–1600)." *Journal of the History of Medicine,* 2 (1947), 451–80.

354 KOYRÉ, A. *From the Closed World to the Infinite Universe.* Baltimore: Johns Hopkins Press, 1957; New York: Harper, 1958.

355 KOYRÉ, A. *The Astronomical Revolution: Copernicus-Kepler-Borelli,* trans. R. E. W. Maddison. Ithaca: Cornell University Press, 1973.

356 KUHN, T. S. *The Copernican Revolution: Planetary Astronomy and the Development of Western Thought.* Cambridge: Harvard University Press, 1957.

357 MANDEL, S. "From the Mummelsee to the Moon: Refractions of Science in Seventeenth-Century Literature." *CLS,* 9 (1972), 407–15.

358 MEADOWS, A. J. *The High Firmament: A Survey of Astronomy in English Literature.* New York: Humanities Press, 1969.

359 NICOLSON, M. H. *Voyages to the Moon.* New York: Macmillan, 1948.

360 ORNSTEIN, M. *The Role of Scientific Societies in the Seventeenth Century.* Chicago: University of Chicago Press, 1928; Hamden: Archon, 1963.

361 PELIKAN, J. "Cosmos and Creation: Science and Theology in Reformation Thought." *PAPS,* 105 (1961), 464–69.

362 PLEDGE, H. T. *Science Since 1500.* New York: Harper, 1959.

363 RHYS, H. H., ed. *Seventeenth-Century Science and the Arts.* Princeton: Princeton University Press, 1966.

364 RULAND, M. *A Lexicon of Alchemy,* trans. A. E. Waite. London: Watkins, 1964.

365 SCHUMAKER, W. *The Occult Sciences in the Renaissance: A Study in Intellectual Patterns.* Berkeley: University of California Press, 1972.

366 SMITH, A. G. R. *Science and Society in the Sixteenth and Seventeenth Centuries.* London: Thames and Hudson, 1972.

367 STIMSON, D. *The Gradual Acceptance of the Copernican Theory of the Universe.* Magnolia: P. Smith, 1972.

368 SYPHER, W. "Similarities between the Scientific and the Historical Revolutions at the End of the Renaissance." *JHI,* 26 (1965), 353—68.

369 TAYLOR, F. S. *The Alchemists: Founders of Modern Chemistry.* New York: Schuman, 1949.

370 THORNDIKE, L. *A History of Magic and Experimental Science,* 8 vols. New York: Columbia University Press, 1923—58

371 WESTFALL, R. S. *Science and Religion in Seventeenth-Century England.* New Haven: Yale University Press, 1958.

372 WHITEHEAD, A. N. *Science and the Modern World.* New York: Macmillan, 1925; Cambridge: Cambridge University Press, 1926; Baltimore: Penguin, 1938.

373 WIGHTMAN, W. P. D. *Science in a Renaissance Society.* New York: Humanities Press, 1972.

374 WOLF, A. *A History of Science, Technology, and Philosophy in the Sixteenth and Seventeenth Centuries.* New York: Macmillan, 1939; New York: Harper, 1959.

Social and Political

375 AKRIGG, G. P. V. *Jacobean Pageant or the Court of King James I.* Cambridge: Harvard University Press, 1962.

376 ALLEN, J. W. *English Political Thought: 1603—1660.* London: Methuen, 1938.

377 ASHLEY, M. P. *England in the Seventeenth Century.* Baltimore: Penguin, 1952.

378 ASHLEY, M. P. *The Greatness of Oliver Cromwell.* London: Hodder & Stoughton, 1957.

379 ASHLEY, M. P. *Life in Stuart England.* New York: Putnam, 1964.

380 BURTON, E. *The Pageant of Stuart England.* New York: Scribner's, 1962.

381 CAMDEN, C. C. *The Elizabethan Woman.* New York, Houston: Elsevier, 1952.

382 CLARK, G. N. *The Seventeenth Century.* Oxford: Clarendon Press, 1929; revised edition, 1947.

383 CLARK, G. N. *The Later Stuarts: 1660—1714.* Oxford: Clarendon Press, 1934, 1955.

384 COOK, O., and A. F. KERSTIG. *The English Country House: An Art and a Way of Life.* London: Thames & Hudson, 1975.

385 COWIE, L. W. *The Trial and Execution of Charles I.* New York: Putnam, 1972.

BACKGROUNDS

386 DAVIES, G. *The Early Stuarts: 1603– 1660.* Oxford: Clarendon Press, 1937, 1959.

387 FINK, Z. S. *The Classical Republicans: An Essay in the Recovery of a Pattern of Thought in Seventeenth-Century England.* Evanston: Northwestern University Press, 1945, 1962.

388 FRASER, A. *King James VI of Scotland and I of England.* New York: Knopf, 1975.

389 GOOCH, G. P. *English Democratic Ideas in the Seventeenth Century.* Cambridge: Cambridge University Press, 1908; revised by H. J. Laski, 1927.

390 GOOCH, G. P. *Political Thought in England from Bacon to Halifax.* London: Butterworth, 1915.

391 GREENLEAF, W. H. *Order, Empiricism, and Politics, 1500– 1700.* Oxford: Oxford University Press, 1964.

392 HART, R. *English Life in the Seventeenth Century.* New York: Putnam, 1970.

393 HEARNSHAW, F. J. C. *The Social and Political Ideas of Some Great Thinkers of the Sixteenth and Seventeenth Centuries.* London: Dawson, 1926, 1967.

394 HIBBERT, C. *Charles I.* New York: Harper & Row, 1968.

395 HILL, C. *Puritanism and Revolution: Studies in Interpretation of the English Revolution of the Seventeenth Century.* London: Secker & Warburg, 1958.

396 HILL, C. *The Century of Revolution, 1603– 1714.* Edinburgh: Nelson, 1961.

397 HILL, C. *Society and Puritanism in Pre-Revolutionary England.* New York: Schocken, 1964.

398 HILL, C. *The Intellectual Origins of the English Revolution.* Oxford: Clarendon Press, 1965.

399 HILL, C. *The Good Old Cause: The English Revolution of 1640– 1660.* London: Cass, 1969.

400 HILL, C. *God's Englishman: Oliver Cromwell and the English Revolution.* New York: Dial, 1970.

401 KELSO, R. *The Doctrine of the English Gentleman.* Urbana: University of Illinois Press, 1929.

402 KELSO, R. *Doctrine for the Lady of the Renaissance.* Urbana: University of Illinois Press, 1956.

403 KNIGHTS, L. C. *Public Voices: Literature and Politics with Special Reference to the Seventeenth Century.* Towata: Rowman & Littlefield, 1972.

404 LOCKYER, R. *Tudor and Stuart Britain, 1471– 1714.* London: Longmans, 1965.

405 MASON, J. E. *Gentlefolk in the Making. Studies in the History of English Courtesy Literature . . . , 1531 to 1774.* Philadelphia: University of Pennsylvania Press, 1935.

406 MATHEW, D. *The Jacobean Age.* London: Green, 1938.

407 MATHEW, D. *The Social Structure in Caroline England.* Oxford: Clarendon Press, 1948.

408 MATHEW, D. *The Age of Charles I.* London: Eyre & Spottiswoode, 1951.

409 MATHEW, D. *James I.* London: Eyre & Spottiswoode, 1967.

BACKGROUNDS

410 McELWEE, W. L. *The Wisest Fool in Christendom: The Reign of King James I and VI.* New York: Harcourt, 1958.

411 PAREL, A., ed. *The Political Calculus: Essays on Machiavelli's Philosophy.* Toronto: University of Toronto Press, 1972.

412 PARKS, G. B. *The English Traveller to Italy.* Rome: Edizioni di Storia e Letteratura, 1954.

413 PENROSE, B. *Tudor and Early Stuart Voyaging.* Washington, D.C.: Folger Shakespeare Library, 1958.

414 RAAB, F. *The English Face of Machiavelli: A Changing Interpretation, 1500–1700.* London: Routledge & Kegan Paul, 1964.

415 REYNOLDS, M. *The Learned Lady in England, 1650–1760.* Boston: Houghton-Mifflin, 1920.

416 SABINE, G. H. *A History of Political Theory.* New York: Holt, 1937; revised editions, 1950, 1954.

417 SMITH, A. G. R., ed. *The Reign of James VI and I.* New York: St. Martin's, 1973.

418 STONE, L. *The Crisis of the Aristocracy, 1558–1641.* New York: Oxford University Press, 1965.

419 STOYE, J. W. *English Travellers Abroad, 1604–1667: Their Influence in English Society and Politics.* London: Cape, 1952.

420 TREVOR-ROPER, H. R. *The Crisis of the Seventeenth Century: Religion, the Reformation, and Social Change.* New York: Harper & Row, 1968.

421 WALZER, M. *The Revolution of the Saints: A Study in the Origins of Radical Politics.* Cambridge: Harvard University Press, 1965.

422 WATSON, D. R. *The Life and Times of Charles I.* London: Weidenfeld & Nicolson, 1972.

423 WEDGWOOD, C. V., et al. *King Charles I.* London: Philip, 1949.

424 WEDGWOOD, C. V. *The Great Rebellion: The King's Peace, 1637–1641.* London: Collins, 1955.

425 WEDGWOOD, C. V. *The Great Rebellion: The King's War, 1641–1647.* London: Collins, 1959.

426 WEDGWOOD, C. V. *A Coffin for King Charles.* New York: Macmillan, 1964.

427 WEDGWOOD, C. V. *Oliver Cromwell.* London: Duckworth, 1973.

428 WILLSON, D. H. *King James VI and I.* New York: Holt, 1956.

429 WRIGHT, L. B. *Middle-Class Culture in Elizabethan England.* Chapel Hill: University of North Carolina Press, 1935; Ithaca: Cornell University Press, 1958.

430 WRIGHT, L. B., and V. A. LAMAR. *Life and Letters in Tudor and Stuart England.* Washington, D.C.: Folger Shakespeare Library, 1958.

Religious

431 ADDLESHAW, G. W. O. *The High-Church Tradition: A Study in the Liturgical Thought of the Seventeenth Century.* London: Faber & Faber, 1941.

432 ADDLESHAW, G. W. O., and F. ETCHELLS. *The Architectural Setting of Anglican Worship.* London: Faber & Faber, 1948.

433 ALEXANDER, H. G. *Religion in England, 1558–1662.* London: University of London Press, 1968.

434 BANGS, C. D. *Arminius.* Nashville: Abingdon, 1971.

435 BICKNELL, E. J. *A Theological Introduction to the Thirty-Nine Articles of the Church of England.* Third edition, revised by H. J. Carpenter. London: Longmans, 1955.

436 BLAU, J. L. *The Christian Interpretation of the Cabala in the Renaissance.* New York: Columbia University Press, 1944.

437 BUTTERFIELD, H. *Christianity and History.* London: Bell, 1949; New York: Scribner's, 1950.

438 BUTTERWORTH, C. C. *The Literary Lineage of the King James Bible, 1340–1611.* Philadelphia: University of Pennsylvania Press, 1941; New York: Octagon, 1971.

439 CARAMAN, P., ed. *The Years of Siege: Catholic Life from James I to Cromwell.* London: Longmans, 1966.

440 CARTER, C. S. *The Anglican Via Media: Being Studies in the Elizabethan Religious Settlement and in the Teaching of the Caroline Divines.* London: Thynne & Jarvis, 1927.

441 COLIE, R. L. *Light and Enlightenment: A Study of the Cambridge Platonists and the Dutch Arminians.* Cambridge: Cambridge University Press, 1957.

442 CRAGG, G. R. "The Collapse of Militant Puritanism." *Essays in Modern Church History,* ed. G. V. Bennett and J. D. Walsh. New York: Oxford University Press, 1966.

443 DAICHES, D. *The King James Version of the English Bible.* Chicago: University of Chicago Press, 1941; Hamden: Archon, 1968.

444 DePAULEY, W. C. *The Candle of the Lord: Studies in the Cambridge Platonists.* New York: Macmillan, 1937.

445 EAKER, J. G. "The Spirit of Seventeenth-Century Anglicanism." *SCB,* 33 (1973), 194–96.

446 ELLIOTT, M. E. *The Language of the King James Bible: A Glossary Explaining Its Words and Expressions.* Garden City: Doubleday, 1967.

447 FRYE, R. M. "The Teaching of Classical Puritanism on Conjugal Love." *SRen,* 2 (1955), 148-59.

448 GEORGE, C. H. and K. G. *The Protestant Mind of the English Reformation, 1570–1640.* Princeton: Princeton University Press, 1961.

449 GREENSLADE, S. L., ed. *The Cambridge History of the Bible,* Vol. 3: *The West from the Reformation to the Present Day.* Cambridge: Cambridge University Press, 1963.

BACKGROUNDS

450 HALLER, W. *The Rise of Puritanism.* New York: Columbia University Press, 1938; New York: Harper, 1957.

451 HALLER, W. *Liberty and Reformation in the Puritan Revolution.* New York: Columbia University Press, 1955.

452 HALLER, W. and M. "The Puritan Art of Love." *HLQ,* 5 (1941—42), 235—72.

453 HARRIS, V. "Allegory to Analogy in the Interpretation of Scripture." *PQ,* 45 (1966), 1—23.

454 HARRISON, A. H. W. *Arminianism.* London: Duckworth, 1937.

455 HAVRAN, M. J. *The Catholics in Caroline England.* Stanford: Stanford University Press, 1962.

456 HENDRY, G. S. *The Westminster Confession.* Richmond: John Knox Press, 1968.

457 HILL, C. *Antichrist in Seventeenth-Century England.* New York: Oxford University Press, 1971.

458 HUGHES, P. *Rome and the Counter-Reformation in England.* London: Burns, Oates, 1942.

459 JANELLE, P. *English Devotional Literature in the Sixteenth and Seventeenth Centuries. English Studies Today: Second Series,* [11], ed. G. A. Bonnard. Bern: Francke Verlag, 1961.

460 JONES, R. M. *Spiritual Reformers in the Sixteenth and Seventeenth Centuries.* New York: Macmillan, 1914, 1959.

461 JORDAN, W. K. *The Development of Religious Toleration in England.* Cambridge: Harvard University Press, 1932—40.

462 MacLURE, M. *The Paul's Cross Sermons, 1534— 1642.* Toronto: University of Toronto Press, 1958.

463 McADOO, H. R. *The Structure of Caroline Moral Theology.* London: Longmans, Green, 1949.

464 McADOO, H. R. *The Spirit of Anglicanism: A Survey of Anglican Theological Method in the Seventeenth Century.* New York: Scribner's, 1965.

465 McNEILL, J. T. *The History and Character of Calvinism.* New York: Oxford University Press, 1954, 1962.

466 McNEILL, J. T. *A History of the Cure of Souls.* New York: Harper, 1951.

467 MILLER, P. *The New England Mind: The Seventeenth Century.* Cambridge: Harvard University Press, 1939, 1954.

468 MILLER, P., and T. H. JOHNSON, eds. *The Puritans: A Sourcebook of Their Writings.* New York: Harper & Row, 1963.

469 MITCHELL, W. F. *English Pulpit Oratory from Andrewes to Tillotson.* New York: Macmillan, 1932; New York: Russell & Russell, 1962.

470 MORE, P. E., and F. L. CROSS, eds. *Anglicanism: The Thought and Practice of the Church of England, Illustrated from the Religious Literature of the Seventeenth Century.* London: S. P. C. K., 1935, etc.; New York: Macmillan, 1957, etc.

471 MORISON, S. *English Prayer Books: An Introduction to the Literature of Christian Public Worship.* Third edition; Cambridge: Cambridge University Press, 1949.

BACKGROUNDS

472 NEW, J. F. H. *Anglican and Puritan: The Basis of Their Opposition, 1558– 1640.* Stanford: Stanford University Press, 1964.

473 PAINE, G. S. *The Learned Man:* [*Translators of the King James Bible*]. New York: Crowell, 1959.

474 PATRIDES, C. A. *The Grand Design of God: The Literary Form of the Christian View of History.* Toronto: University of Toronto Press, 1972.

475 PETTIT, N. *The Heart Prepared: Grace and Conversion in Puritan Spiritual Life.* New Haven: Yale University Press, 1966.

476 REEVES, M. "History and Eschatology: Medieval and Early Protestant Thought in Some English and Scottish Writings." *M & H,* 4 (1973), 99– 123.

477 ROBINSON, H. W. *The Bible in its Ancient and English Versions.* Oxford: Clarendon Press, 1940.

478 ROSS, K. N. *The Thirty-Nine Articles.* London: Mowbray; New York: Morehouse-Gorham, 1957.

479 RYAN, J. K. "The Reputation of St. Thomas Aquinas among English Protestant Thinkers of the Seventeenth Century." *New Scholasticism,* 22 (1948), 1–33, 126–208.

480 STRANKS, C. J. *Anglican Devotion: Studies in the Spiritual Life of the Church of England between the Reformation and the Oxford Movement.* London: SCM Press, 1961.

481 THOMPSON, C. R. *The Bible in English, 1525– 1611.* Washington, D.C.: Folger Shakespeare Library, 1958.

482 TULLOCH, J. *Rational Theology and Christian Philosophy in England in the Seventeenth Century.* Edinburgh: Blackwood, 1872, etc.

483 WALKER, D. P. *The Decline of Hell: Seventeenth-Century Discussions of Eternal Torment.* Chicago: University of Chicago Press, 1964.

484 WATKINS, O. C. *The Puritan Experience: Studies in Spiritual Autobiography.* New York: Schocken, 1971.

485 WHITE, E. E. *Puritan Rhetoric: The Issue of Emotion in Religion.* Carbondale: Southern Illinois University Press, 1972.

486 WHITE, H. C. *English Devotional Literature, 1600– 1640.* Madison: University of Wisconsin Press, 1931; New York: Haskell House, 1966.

487 WILLIAMS, A. *The Common Expositor: An Account of the Commentaries on Genesis, 1527– 1633.* Chapel Hill: University of North Carolina Press, 1948.

488 WILSON, J. F. *Pulpit in Parliament: Puritanism during the English Civil Wars, 1640– 1648.* Princeton: Princeton University Press, 1969.

489 WOLF, E., II. "The Bible in Transition." *PULC,* 24 (1963), 155–67.

Individual Authors

Lancelot Andrewes (1555— 1626)

Editions

490 *Complete Works,* ed. J. P. Wilson and J. Bliss, 11 vols. Oxford: Parker, 1841—54; New York: AMS Press, 1967.

491 *The Devotions,* trans. J. H. Newman and J. M. Neale. London: S.P.C.K., 1920.

492 *The Private Devotions . . . : Preces Privatae,* ed. F. E. Brightman. London: Methuen, 1949; New York: Meridian, 1961.

493 *The Private Devotions,* ed. T. S. Kepler. Cleveland: World Publishing, 1957.

494 *The Private Devotions,* ed. D. A. MacLennan. New York: World Publishing, 1969.

495 *The Private Prayers,* ed. H. Martin. London: SCM Press, 1957.

496 *Sermons,* selected and ed. G. M. Story. Oxford: Clarendon Press, 1967.

497 *Sermons on The Nativity.* Grand Rapids: Baker Book House, 1955.

Studies

498 ELIOT, T. S. "Lancelot Andrewes." See **86.**

499 HIGHAM, F. *Lancelot Andrewes.* London: SCM Press, 1952.

500 MACLEANE, D. *Lancelot Andrewes and the Reaction.* London: Allen, 1910.

501 McCUTCHEON, E. "Lancelot Andrewes' *Preces Privatae:* A Journey Through Time." *SP,* (1968), 223—41.

502 MITCHELL, W. F. *English Pulpit Oratory.* See **469.**

503 REIDY, M. *Bishop Lancelot Andrewes, Jacobean Court Preacher: A Study in Early Seventeenth-Century Religious Thought.* Chicago: Loyola University Press, 1955.

504 STORY, G. M. "The Text of Lancelot Andrewes's Sermons." See **283.**

505 WEBBER, J. "Celebration of Word and World in Lancelot Andrewes' Style." *JEGP,* 64 (1965), 255—69; and see **276.**

506 WELSBY, P. A. *Lancelot Andrewes, 1555— 1626.* London: S.P.C.K., 1958.

Francis Bacon (1561– 1626)

Editions

507 *The Works,* ed. J. Spedding, R. L. Ellis, and D. D. Heath. London: Longman, 1858–74, etc.; Boston: Brown and Taggart, 1900; New York: Garrett, 1968.

508 *The Philosophical Works,* with notes and prefaces by R. L. Ellis and J. Spedding, ed. J. M. Robertson. London: Routledge, 1905, etc.

509 *Selected Writings,* ed. H. G. Dick. New York: Modern Library, 1955.

510 *Selected,* ed. A. Johnston. New York: Schocken, 1965.

511 *Selections,* ed. M. T. McLure. New York: Scribner's, 1928.

512 *A Selection of His Works,* ed. S. Warhaft. New York: St. Martin's, 1965.

513 *Complete Essays . . . , The New Atlantis, and Novum Organum,* ed. H. L. Finch. New York: Washington Square, 1963.

514 *Essays, Advancement of Learning, New Atlantis, and Other Pieces,* ed. R. F. Jones. Garden City: Doubleday, 1937.

515 *The Advancement of Learning, and The New Atlantis,* ed. T. Case. London: Oxford University Press, 1913, etc.

516 *The Advancement of Learning,* ed. A. Johnston. London: Dent, 1973; Towata: Roman & Littlefield, 1973.

517 *The Advancement of Learning,* ed. G. W. Kitchen. London: Dent, 1915, etc.; New York: Dutton, 1958.

518 *The Advancement of Learning,* ed. F. G. Selby. New York: St. Martin's, 1964.

519 *The Advancement of Learning,* ed. W. A. Wright. Third edition, revised; Oxford: Clarendon Press, 1885, etc.

520 *Apophthegmes, New and Old.* New York: DaCapo, 1972.

521 *Essays.* London: Oxford University Press, 1955.

522 *Essays.* Mount Vernon: Peter Pauper Press, 1963.

523 *Selected Essays,* ed. J. M. Patrick. Arlington Heights: AHM Publishing Corporation, 1948, etc.

524 *Essays,* ed. O. Smeaton. London: Dent, 1906, etc.

525 *Essays,* ed. F. G. Selby. New York: St. Martin's, 1964.

526 *Essays,* ed. A. S. West. Cambridge: Cambridge University Press, 1920.

527 *Essays, and Colours of Good and Evil,* ed. W. A. Wright. London: Macmillan, 1862, etc.; Freeport: Books for Libraries, 1972.

528 *New Atlantis,* ed. H. Osborne. London: University Tutorial Press, 1969.

529 *The History of Henry VII,* ed. J. Devey. London: Bell & Sons, 1874.

530 *The History of the Reign of King Henry VII,* ed. F. J. Levy. New York: Bobbs-Merrill, 1972.

531 *The New Organon, and Related Writings,* ed. F. H. Anderson, New York: Liberal Arts Press, 1960.

532 *The Wisdome of the Ancients.* Amsterdam: Theatrum Orbis Terrarum, 1968.

533 *The Wisdome of the Ancients.* New York: Da Capo, 1968.

Bibliography and Concordances

535 ARBER, E. *A Harmony of the Essays.* London: By the author 1971; New York: AMS Press, 1966.

536 DAVIES, D. W., and E. S. WRIGLEY, eds. *A Concordance to the "Essays" of Francis Bacon.* Detroit: Gale Research Co., 1973.

537 HOUCK, J. K., ed. *Elizabethan Bibliographies Supplements, 15: Francis Bacon, 1925–1966.* London: Nether Press, 1968.

Comprehensive Studies

538 ANDERSON, F. H. *The Philosophy of Francis Bacon.* Chicago: University of Chicago Press, 1948; New York: Octagon, 1971.

539 ANDERSON, F. H. *Francis Bacon: His Career and His Thought.* Los Angeles: University of Southern California Press, 1962.

540 BOAS, M. "Bacon and Gilbert." *JHI,* 12 (1951), 466–67.

541 BOWEN, C. D. *Francis Bacon: The Temper of a Man.* Boston: Little, Brown, 1963.

542 BROAD, C. D. "Francis Bacon and the Scientific Method." *Nature,* 118 (1926), 481–88, 523–24.

543 BROAD, C. D. *The Philosophy of Francis Bacon.* Cambridge: Cambridge University Press, 1926.

544 BULLOUGH, G. "Bacon and the Defence of Learning." See **123.**

545 BUNDY, M. W. "Bacon's True Opinion of Poetry." *SP,* 27 (1930), 244–64.

546 BURKE, P. B. "Rhetorical Considerations of Bacon's Style." *CCC,* 18 (1967), 23–31.

547 COCHRANE, R. C. "Francis Bacon and the Architect of Fortune." *SRen,* 5 (1958), 176-95.

548 COCHRANE, R. C. "Francis Bacon in Early Eighteenth-Century English Literature." *PQ,* 37 (1958), 58–79.

549 CREETH, E. H. "Bacon's Humanism." *PMASAL,* 47 (1962), 637–48.

550 CROWTHER, J. G. *Francis Bacon: The First Statesman of Science.* London: Cresset Press, 1960.

551 DAVIS, W. "The Imagery of Bacon's Late Work." *MLQ,* 27 (1966), 255–73.

552 EISELEY, L. *Francis Bacon and the Modern Dilemma.* Lincoln: University of Nebraska Press, 1962.

553 FARRINGTON, B. *Francis Bacon: Philosopher of Industrial Science.* New York: Schuman, 1949; New York: Collier Books, 1961; New York: Haskell House, 1973.

554 FARRINGTON, B. *The Philosophy of Francis Bacon: An Essay on His Development from 1603– 1609, with New Translations of Fundamental Texts.* Liverpool: Liverpool University Press, 1964; Chicago: Chicago University Press, 1967.

555 FARRINGTON, B. "Francis Bacon After His Fall." *SLitI,* 4 (1971), 143–58.

556 FISCH, H., and H. W. JONES. "Bacon's Influence on Sprat's *History of the Royal Society.*" *MLQ,* 13 (1951), 399–406.

557 GARNER, B. C. "Francis Bacon, Natalis Comes, and the Mythological Tradition." *JWCI,* 33 (1970), 264–91.

558 GREEN, A. W. *Sir Francis Bacon: His Life and Works.* Syracuse: Syracuse University Press, 1948; Denver: Swallow, 1952.

559 GREEN, A. W. *Sir Francis Bacon.* New York: Twayne, 1966.

560 HALL, M. B. "In Defense of Bacon's Views on the Reform of Science." *Person,* 44 (1963), 437–53.

561 HARRISON, J. L. "Bacon's View of Rhetoric, Poetry, and the Imagination." *HLQ,* 20 (1957), 107–25.

562 JAMES, D. G. *The Dream of Learning: An Essay on "The Advancement of Learning," "Hamlet," and "King Lear."* New York: Oxford University Press, 1951.

563 JAMESON, T. H. *Francis Bacon: Criticism and the Modern World.* New York: Praeger, 1954.

564 JARDINE, L. *Francis Bacon: Discovery and the Art of Discourse.* Cambridge: Cambridge University Press, 1975.

565 JONES, R. F. "The Bacon of the Seventeenth Century." See **352.**

567 KELLY, H. A. "The Deployment of Faith and Reason in Bacon's Approach to Knowledge." *Modern Schoolman,* 42 (1965), 265–85.

568 KNIGHTS, L. C. "Bacon and the Seventeenth-Century Dissociation of Sensibility." See **104.**

569 KOCHER, P. H. "Francis Bacon on the Science of Jurisprudence." *JHI,* 18 (1957), 3–26.

570 KOCHER, P. H. "Francis Bacon on the Drama." *Essays on Shakespeare and the Elizabethan Drama in Honor of Hardin Craig,* ed. R. Hosley. Columbia: University of Missouri Press, 1962.

571 LARSEN, R. E. "The Aristotelianism of Bacon's *Novum Organum.*" *JHI,* 23 (1962), 435–50.

572 LEMMI, C. W. *The Classic Deities in Bacon.* Baltimore: Johns Hopkins Press, 1933.

573 LEVINE, I. E. *Francis Bacon.* Boston: Small, Maynard, 1925; Port Washington: Kennikat, 1970.

574 LINDEN, S. J. "Francis Bacon and Alchemy: The Reformation of Vulcan." *JHI,* 35 (1974), 547–60.

575 MARGENEAU, H. "Bacon and Modern Physics: A Confrontation." *PAPS,* 105 (1961), 487–92.

576 MAZZEO, J. A. "Bacon: The New Philosophy." See **111.**

577 McCABE, B. "Francis Bacon and the Natural Law Tradition." *Natural Law Forum,* 9 (1964), 111 – 21.

578 McCREARY, E. P. "Bacon's Theory of Imagination Reconsidered." *HLQ,* 36 (1973), 317 – 26.

579 McNAMEE, M. B. "Literary Decorum in Francis Bacon." *Saint Louis University Studies, Series A,* 1 (1950), 1 – 52.

580 McNAMEE, M. B. "Bacon's Inductive Method and Humanistic Grammar." *SLitI,* 4 (1971), 81 – 106.

581 McRAE, R. "The Unity of the Sciences: Bacon, Descartes, and Leibniz." *JHI,* 18 (1957), 27 – 48.

583 PATERSON, A. M. *Francis Bacon and Socialized Science.* Springfield: Thomas, 1973.

584 PATRICK, J. M. *Francis Bacon.* London, New York: Longmans, Green, 1961.

585 PATRICK, J. M. "Hawk Versus Dove: Francis Bacon's Advocacy of a Holy War . . . Against the Turks." *SLitI,* 4 (1971), 159 – 71.

586 PRIOR, M. E. "Bacon's Man of Science." *JHI,* 15 (1954), 348 – 70.

587 ROSSI, P. *Francis Bacon: From Magic to Science.* London: Routledge & Kegan Paul, 1968.

588 SESSIONS, W. A. "Francis Bacon and the Negative Instance." *RenP* (1970), 1 – 9.

589 SEWELL, E. "Bacon, Vico, Coleridge, and Poetic Method." *Giambatista Vico: An International Symposium,* ed. G. Tagliacozzi and H. V. White. Baltimore: Johns Hopkins Press, 1969.

590 STEADMAN, J. M. "Beyond Hercules: Bacon and the Scientist as Hero." *SLitI,* 4 (1971), 3 – 47.

591 STEPHENS, J. "Science and the Aphorism: Bacon's Theory of the Philosophical Style." *SM,* 37 (1970), 157 – 71.

592 STEPHENS, J. "Bacon's Fable-Making: A Strategy of Style." *SEL,* 14 (1974), 112 – 27.

593 THORNDIKE, L. "The Attitude of Francis Bacon and Descartes Towards Magic and Occult Science." *Science, Medicine, and History: Essays . . . in Honour of Charles Singer,* ed. E. A. Underwood. New York: Oxford University Press, 1954.

594 TREVOR-ROPER, H. "Francis Bacon." *Encounter,* 18 (1962), 73 – 77.

595 VICKERS, B., ed. *Essential Articles for the Study of Francis Bacon.* Hamden: Shoestring Press, 1969.

596 VICKERS, B. *Francis Bacon and Renaissance Prose.* London: Cambridge University Press, 1968.

597 VICKERS, B. "Bacon's Use of Theatrical Imagery." *SLitI,* 4 (1971), 189 – 226.

598 WALLACE, K. R. *Francis Bacon on Communication and Rhetoric.* Chapel Hill: University of North Carolina Press, 1943.

599 WALLACE, K. R. "Bacon's Conception of Rhetoric." *Historical Studies of Rhetoric and Rhetoricians,* ed. R. F. Howes. Ithaca: Cornell University Press, 1961.

600 WALLACE, K. R. *Francis Bacon on the Nature of Man.* Urbana: University of Illinois Press, 1968.

601 WALLACE, K. R. "Francis Bacon on Understanding, Reason, and Rhetoric." *SM,* 38 (1971), 111 – 18.

602 WALLACE, K. R. "Chief Guides for the Study of Bacon's Speeches." *SLitI,* 4 (1971), 173 – 88.

603 WALLACE, K. R. "Francis Bacon and Method: Theory and Practice." *SM,* 40 (1973), 243 – 72.

604 WARHAFT, S. "Science against Man in Bacon." *BuR,* 7 (1958), 158 – 73.

605 WARHAFT, S. "The Anomaly of Bacon's Allegorizing." *PMASAL,* 43 (1958), 327 – 33.

606 WARHAFT, S. "Bacon and the Renaissance Ideal of Self-Knowledge." *Person,* 44 (1963), 454 – 71.

607 WARHAFT, S. "The Providential Order in Bacon's New Philosophy." *SLitI,* 4 (1971), 49 – 64.

608 WHEELER, T. V. "Sir Francis Bacon in the Laboratory." *TSL,* 9 (1964), 49 – 55.

609 WHITAKER, V. K. *Francis Bacon's Intellectual Milieu.* Los Angeles: University of Southern California Press, 1962.

610 WHITAKER, V. K. "Bacon's Doctrine of Forms: A Study of Seventeenth-Century Eclecticism." *HLQ,* 33 (1970), 209 – 16.

611 WHITAKER, V. K. "Francesco Patrizi and Francis Bacon." *SLitI,* 4 (1971), 107 – 20.

612 WHITE, H. B. *Peace among the Willows: The Political Philosophy of Francis Bacon.* The Hague: Nijhoff, 1968.

613 WHITEHEAD, A. N. See **372.**

614 WILEY, M. L. "Francis Bacon: Induction and/or Rhetoric." *SLitI,* 4 (1971), 65 – 79.

615 WILLEY, B. "Bacon and the Rehabilitation of Nature." See **136.**

Studies: Specific Works

Essays

616 CRANE, R. S. "The Relation of Bacon's *Essays* to his Program for the Advancement of Learning." *Schelling Anniversary Papers.* New York: Century, 1923.

617 FISH, S. E. "Georgics of the Mind: Bacon's Philosophy and the Experience of His Essays." *English Literature and British Philosophy,* ed. S. P. Rosenbaum. Chicago: of Chicago Press, 1971. See **88** and **276.**

618 THOMPSON, E. N. S. *The Seventeenth-Century English Essay.* Iowa City: University of Iowa Press, 1928.

619 TILLOTSON, G. "Words for Princes: Bacon's Essays." *Essays in Criticism and Research.* Cambridge: Cambridge University Press, 1942.

620 ZEITLIN, J. "The Development of Bacon's Essays." *JEGP,* 27 (1928), 496–519.

Henry VII

621 BERRY, E. I. "History and Rhetoric in Bacon's *Henry VII.*" See **276.**

622 DEAN, L. F. "Sir Francis Bacon's Theory of Civil History Writing." *ELH,* 8 (1944), 161–83.

623 KIRKWOOD, J. J. "Bacon's *Henry VII;* A Model of a Theory of History." *RenP* (1965), 51–55.

624 SCHUSTER, Sr. M. F. "Philosophy of Life and Prose Style in Thomas More's *Richard III* and Francis Bacon's *Henry VII.*" *PMLA,* 70 (1955), 474–87.

625 WHEELER, T. V. "Sir Francis Bacon's Concept of the Historian's Task." *RenP* (1955), 40–46.

626 WHEELER, T. V. "The Purpose of Bacon's *History of Henry the Seventh.*" *SP,* 54 (1957), 1–13.

627 WHEELER, T. V. "Bacon's Henry VII as Machiavellian Prince." *RenP* (1958), 111–17.

628 WHEELER, T. V. "Sir Francis Bacon's Historical Imagination." *TSL,* 14 (1969), 111–18.

New Atlantis

629 ADAMS, R. P. "The Social Responsibilities of Science in *Utopia, New Atlantis* and After." *JHI,* 10 (1949), 374–98.

630 BIERMAN, J. "Science and Society in the *New Atlantis* and Other Renaissance Utopias." *PMLA,* 78 (1963), 492–500.

631 BIERMAN, J. "The *New Atlantis,* Bacon's Utopia of Science." *PLL,* 3 (1967), 99–110.

632 BIERMAN, J. "*New Atlantis* Revisited." *SLitI,* 4 (1971), 121–41.

633 COLIE, R. L. "Cornelius Drebel and Salomon de Caus: Two Jacobean Models for Salomon's House." *HLQ,* 18 (1955), 245–60.

634 McCUTCHEON, E. "Bacon and the Cherubim: An Iconographical Reading of the *New Atlantis.*" *ELR,* 2 (1972), 334–55.

635 SUTER, R. "Salomon's House: A Study of Francis Bacon." *Scientific Monthly,* 66 (1948), 62–66.

636 WIENER, H. S. "Science or Providence: Toward Knowledge in Bacon's *New Atlantis.*" *EnlE,* 3 (1972), 85–92.

Thomas Browne (1605–1682)

Editions

637 *The Works,* ed. G. Keynes, 4 vols., second edition. Chicago: University of Chicago Press, 1964.

638 *The Prose,* ed. N. J. Endicott. Garden City: Doubleday, 1967.

639 *Selected Writings,* ed. G. Keynes. Chicago: University of Chicago Press, 1968.

640 *Christian Morals,* ed. S. C. Roberts. Cambridge: Cambridge University Press, 1927; New York: Kraus Reprint, 1969.

641 *Religio Medici and Other Writings,* ed. F. L. Huntley. New York: Dutton, 1951.

642 *Religio Medici and Other Works,* ed. L. C. Martin, Oxford: Clarendon Press, 1964.

643 *Religio Medici and Other Writings,* ed. H. Sutherland. London: Dent, 1956.

644 *Religio Medici, Hydriotaphia, and The Garden of Cyrus,* ed. R. H. A. Robbins. Oxford: Clarendon Press, 1972.

645 *Religio Medici,* ed. J-J Denonain. Cambridge: Cambridge University Press, 1953.

646 *Religio Medici,* ed. F. L. Huntley. Arlington Heights: AHM Publishing Corp., 1966.

647 *Religio Medici,* ed. J. Winny. Cambridge: Cambridge University Press, 1963.

648 *Hydriotaphia (Urn Burial) and The Garden of Cyrus,* ed. F. L. Huntley. Arlington Heights: AHM Publishing Corp., 1966.

649 *Urne Burial and The Garden of Cyrus,* ed. J. Carter. Cambridge: Cambridge University Press, 1958, 1967.

Bibliographies

650 DONOVAN, D. G., ed. *Elizabethan Bibliographies Supplements, 10: Sir Thomas Browne, 1924–1966.* London: Nether Press, 1968.

651 DONOVAN, D. G., ed. "Recent Studies in Browne." *ELR,* 2 (1972), 271–79.

652 KEYNES, G., ed. *A Bibliography of Sir Thomas Browne, Kt., M.D.* second edition, revised. Oxford: Clarendon Press, 1968.

Studies

653 BENNETT, J. "A Note on *Religio Medici* and Some of Its Critics." *SRen,* 3 (1956), 175—84.

654 BENNETT, J. *Sir Thomas Browne.* Cambridge: Cambridge University Press, 1962.

655 BOTTRALL, M. "Browne's *Religio Medici.*" See **269.**

656 CAWLEY, R. R., and G. YOST. *Studies in Sir Thomas Browne.* Eugene: University of Oregon Press, 1965.

657 CHALMERS, G. K. "Hieroglyphics and Sir Thomas Browne." *VQR,* 11 (1935), 547—60.

658 CHALMERS, G. K. " 'That Universal and Publick Manuscript.' " *VQR,* 26 (1950), 414—30.

659 CLINE, J. M. *"Hydriotaphia." Five Studies in Literature.* Berkeley: University of California Pdress, 1940.

660 CURRIE, H. M. "Notes on Sir Thomas Browne's *Christian Morals.*" *N&Q,* 5 (1958), 143.

661 DUNN, W. P. *Sir Thomas Browne: A Study in Religious Philosophy.* Minneapolis: University of Minnesota Press, 1950.

662 ENDICOTT, N. J. "Some Aspects of Self-Revelation and Self-Portraiture in *Religio Medici." Essays in English Literature from the Renaissance to the Victorian Age,* ed. M. MacLure and F. W. Watt. Toronto: University of Toronto Press, 1964.

663 FINCH, J. S. "Sir Thomas Browne and the Quinqunx." *SP,* 37 (1940), 274—82.

664 FINCH, J. S. *Sir Thomas Browne: A Doctor's Life of Science and Faith.* New York: Schumann, 1950.

665 FISH, S. "The Bad Physician: The Case of Sir Thomas Browne." See **88.**

666 GREEN, P. *Sir Thomas Browne.* London, New York: Longmans, Green, 1959.

667 GRUNDY, D. "Skepticism in Two Essays by Montaigne and Sir Thomas Browne." *JHI,* 34 (1973), 529—42.

668 HEIDEMAN, M. A. *"Hydriotaphia* and *The Garden of Cyrus:* A Paradox and a Cosmic Vision." *UTQ,* 19 (1949—50), 235—46.

669 HOWELL, A. C. "Sir Thomas Browne and Seventeenth-Century Scientific Thought." *SP,* 22 (1925), 61—80.

670 HOWELL, A. C. "A Note on Sir Thomas Browne's Knowledge of Languages." *SP,* 22 (1925), 412—17.

671 HOWELL, A. C. "Sir Thomas Browne as Wit and Humorist." *SP,* 42 (1945), 564—77.

672 HUNTLEY, F. L. "Sir Thomas Browne, M. D., William Harvey, and the Metaphor of the Circle." *Bulletin of the History of Medicine,* 25 (1951), 236—47.

673 HUNTLEY, F. L. "Sir Thomas Browne and the Metaphor of the Circle." *JHI*, 14 (1953), 353 – 64.

674 HUNTLEY, F. L. "The Publication and Immediate Reception of *Religio Medici*." *Library Quarterly*, 25 (1955), 203 – 18.

675 HUNTLEY, F. L. "Sir Thomas Browne: The Relationship of *Urn Burial* and *The Garden of Cyrus*." *SP*, 53 (1956), 204 – 19; and see **276.**

676 HUNTLEY, F. L. *Sir Thomas Browne: A Biographical and Critical Study.* Ann Arbor: University of Michigan Press, 1962.

677 JAFFE, M. "Sir Thomas Browne at Midnight: [*The Garden of Cyrus*]." *Cambridge Journal*, 2 (1949), 752 – 57.

678 MACKENZIE, N. "Sir Thomas Browne as a Man of Learning: A Discussion of *Urn Burial* and *The Garden of Cyrus*." *ESA*, 10 (1967), 67 – 86.

680 MERTON, E. S. "Sir Thomas Browne's Scientific Quest [in *Pseudodoxia Epidemica*]." *Journal of the History of Medicine*, 3 (1948), 214 – 28.

681 MERTON, E. S. "Sir Thomas Browne's Interpretation of Dreams." *PQ*, 28 (1949), 497 – 503.

682 MERTON, E. S. "Sir Thomas Browne's Embryological Theory." *Journal of the History of Medicine*, 5 (1950), 416 – 21.

683 MERTON, E. S. "Microcosm, Epitome, and Seed: Some Seventeenth-Century Analogies. *HINL*, 3 (1957), 54 – 57.

684 MERTON, E. S. "Sir Thomas Browne on Astronomy." *HINL*, 4 (1958), 83 – 86.

685 MERTON, E. S. *Science and Imagination in Sir Thomas Browne.* New York: King's Crown Press, 1949; New York: Octagon, 1969.

686 MOLONEY, M. F. "Metre and *Cursus* in Sir Thomas Browne's Prose." *JEGP*, 58 (1959), 60 – 67.

687 NATHANSON, L. " *Urne Burial* and the Ethics of Mortality." See **276.**

688 NATHANSON, L. *The Strategy of Truth: A Study of Sir Thomas Browne.* Chicago: University of Chicago Press, 1967.

689 PARKER, E. L. "The *Cursus* in Sir Thomas Browne." *PMLA*, 53 (1938), 1037 – 53.

690 PHELPS, G. "The Prose of . . . Browne." See **7.**

691 SCHNECK, J. M. "Sir Thomas Browne, *Religio Medici*, and the History of Psychiatry." *American Journal of Psychiatry*, 114 (1958), 657 – 60.

692 STAPLETON, L. "Sir Thomas Browne and Meditative Prose." See **284.**

693 TEMPEST, N. "Rhythm in the Prose of Sir Thomas Browne." *RES*, 3 (1927), 308 – 18.

694 THALER, A. "Sir Thomas Browne and the Elizabethans." *SP*, 28 (1931), 87 – 117.

695 WARREN, A. "The Styles of Sir Thomas Browne." *KR*, 13 (1951), 674 – 87; and see **276.**

696 WEBBER, J. "Sir Thomas Browne: Art as Recreation." See **287.**

697 WHALLON, W. "Hebraic Synonymy in Sir Thomas Browne." *ELH,* 28 (1961), 335—52.

698 WILEY, M. L. "Sir Thomas Browne and the Genesis of Paradox." *JHI,* 9 (1948), 303—22.

699 WILLEY, B. "Sir Thomas Browne." See **136.**

700 WILLIAMSON, G. "The Purple of *Urn Burial." MP,* 62 (1964), 110—17; and see **139.**

701 WILSON, F. P. "Sir Thomas Browne." See **290.**

702 WISE, J. N. *Sir Thomas Browne's "Religio Medici" and Two Seventeenth-Century Critics.* Columbia: University of Missouri Press, 1973.

703 ZIEGLER, D. K. *In Divided and Distinguished Worlds: Religion and Rhetoric in the Writings of Sir Thomas Browne.* Cambridge: Harvard University Press, 1943.

Robert Burton (1577— 1640)

Editions

704 *The Anatomy of Melancholy,* ed. A. R. Shilleto. London: Bell, 1893, 1903, 1926.

705 *The Anatomy of Melancholy,* ed. H. Jackson. London: Dent; New York: Dutton, 1932.

706 *The Anatomy of Melancholy,* ed. F. Dell and P. Jordan-Smith. New York: Tudor, 1941, 1951.

707 *The Anatomy of Melancholy (A Selection),* ed. L. Babb. East Lansing: Michigan State University Press, 1965.

709 *Burton the Anatomist: Extracts,* ed. G. C. F. Mead and R. C. Clift. London: Methuen, 1925.

710 *Philophaster,* ed. P. J. Smith. Stanford: Stanford University Press, 1931.

Bibliographies

711 DONOVAN, D. G., ed. *Elizabethan Bibliographies Supplements, 10; . . . Robert Burton, 1924— 1966.* London: Nether Press, 1968.

712 DONOVAN, D., ed. "Recent Studies in Burton . . . ." *ELR,* 1 (1971), 294—303.

713 JORDAN-SMITH, P., and M. MULHAUSER, eds. *Burton's Anatomy of Melancholy and Burtoniana: A Checklist.* New York: Oxford University Press, 1959.

714 JORDAN-SMITH, P. *Bibliographia Burtoniana.* See **730.**

Studies

715 BABB, L. "On the Nature of Elizabethan Psychological Literature." *J. Q. Adams Memorial Studies,* ed. J. McManaway, G. Dawson, and E. Willoughby. Washington, D.C.: Folger Shakespeare Library, 1948.

716 BABB, L. *Sanity in Bedlam: A Study of Robert Burton's "Anatomy of Melancholy."* East Lansing: Michigan State University Press, 1959.

717 BABB, L. *The Elizabethan Malady.* See **72.**

718 BARLOW, R. G. "Infinite Worlds: Robert Burton's Cosmic Voyage." *JHI,* 34 (1973), 291 – 302.

719 BEUM, R. "The Scientific Affinities of English Baroque Prose." *EM,* 13 (1962), 59 – 80.

720 BLACK, E. L. "Burton the Anatomist." *English,* 7 (1949), 266 – 70.

721 BROWNE, R. M. "Robert Burton and the New Cosmology." *MLQ,* 13 (1952), 131 – 48.

722 COLIE, R. L. "Some Notes on Burton's Erasmus." *RenQ,* 20 (1967), 335 – 41.

723 COLIE, R. L. "Burton's *Anatomy of Melancholy* and the Structure of Paradox." See **79** and **276.**

724 DEWEY, N. " 'Democritus Junior,' Alias Robert Burton." *PULC,* 31 (1970), 103 – 21.

725 DEWEY, N. "Burton's *Melancholy:* A Paradox Disinterred." *MP,* 68 (1971), 292 – 93.

726 DONOVAN, D. G. "Robert Burton, Anglican Minister." *RenP* (1967), 33 – 39.

727 EVANS, B. *The Psychiatry of Robert Burton.* New York: Columbia University Press, 1944; New York: Octagon, 1972.

728 FISH, S. "Thou Thyself Art the Subject of My Discourse: Democritus Jr. to the Reader." See **88.**

729 GOLDSTEIN, L. "Science and Literary Style in Robert Burton's 'Cento out of Divers Writers.' " *JRUL,* 21 (1958), 55 – 68.

730 JORDAN-SMITH, P. *Bibliographia Burtoniana: A Study of Robert Burton's "The Anatomy of Melancholy" with a Bibliography of Burton's Writings.* Stanford: Stanford University Press, 1931.

731 LIEVSAY, J. L. "Robert Burton's *De Consolatione." SAQ,* 55 (1956), 329 – 36.

732 MADAN, F., ed. "Robert Burton and the *Anatomy of Melancholy." Oxford Bibliographical Society Proceedings,* 1, iii (1925), 159 – 246.

733 MUELLER, W. R. "Robert Burton's Economic and Political Views." *HLQ,* 11 (1948), 341 – 59.

734 MUELLER, W. R. "Robert Burton's *Frontispiece* as Illustrative of the Text." *PMLA,* 64 (1949), 1074 – 88.

735 MUELLER, W. R. "Robert Burton's 'Satyrical Preface.' " *MLQ,* 15 (1954), 28 – 35.

736 MUELLER, W. R. *The Anatomy of Robert Burton's England.* Berkeley: University of California Press, 1952.

737 NOCHIMSON, R. L. "Studies in the Life of Robert Burton." *YES*, 4 (1974), 85–111.

738 PATRICK, J. M. "Robert Burton's Utopianism." *PQ*, 27 (1948), 345–58.

739 PUTNEY, R. " 'Our Vegetable Love': Marvel and Burton." See **68.**

740 RENAKER, D. "Robert Burton and Ramist Method." *RenQ*, 24 (1971), 210–20.

741 RENAKER, D. "Robert Burton's Tricks of Memory." *PMLA*, 87 (1972), 391–96.

742 SIMON, J. R. *"Robert Burton (1577–1640) et "L'Anatomie de la melancholie."* Paris: Didier, 1964.

743 WEBBER, J. "The Anatomy of Democritus, Jr." See **287.**

744 WILSON, F. P. "Robert Burton." See **276.**

Thomas Carew (1594– 1640)

Editions

745 *The Poems*, ed. R. Dunlap. Oxford: Clarendon Press, 1949.

746 *Poems*, ed. A. Vincent. New York: Scribner's, 1899; Freeport: Books for Libraries, 1972.

747 [*Selections*], ed. H. N. Maclean. See **47.**

Bibliographies

748 BERRY, L. E., ed. "Thomas Carew: [Bibliography]." See **4.**

749 SPENCER, T., ed. "Thomas Carew: [Bibliography]." See **17.**

Studies

750 BLANSHARD, R. A. "Thomas Carew and the Cavalier Poets." *Transactions of the Wisconsin Academy of Sciences, Arts, and Letters*, 43 (1954), 97–106.

751 BLANSHARD, R. A. "Carew and Jonson." *SP*, 52 (1955), 195–211.

752 BLANSHARD, R. A. "Thomas Carew's Master Figures." *BUSE*, 3 (1957), 214–27.

753 KING, B. "The Strategy of Carew's Wit." *Review of English Literature*, 5 (1964), 42–51; and see **47.**

754 MARTZ, L. L. "Thomas Carew: The Cavalier World." See **209**.

755 PALMER, P. "From Butterfly to Bird of Paradise." *RomN*, 15 (1973), 123−28.

756 PARFITT, G. A. E. "The Poetry of Thomas Carew." *RMS*, 12 (1968), 56−67.

757 RAUBER, D. F. "Carew Redivivus." *TSLL*, 13 (1971), 17−28.

758 SELIG, E. I. *The Flourishing Wreath: A Study of Thomas Carew's Poetry.* New Haven: Yale University Press, 1958.

John Cleveland (1613− 1658)

Editions

759 *The Poems,* ed. J. M. Berdan. New York: Grafton, 1903; New Haven: Yale University Press, 1911.

760 *The Poems,* ed. B. Morris and E. Worthington. New York: Oxford University Press, 1967.

Bibliographies

761 BERRY, L. E., ed. "John Cleveland: [Bibliography]." See **4**.

762 MORRIS, B., ed. *John Cleveland (1613− 1658): A Bibliography of His Poems.* London: Bibliographical Society, 1967.

763 SPENCER, T., ed. "John Cleveland: [Bibliography]." See **17**.

Studies

764 GAPP, S. V. "Notes on John Cleveland." *PMLA*, 46 (1931), 1075−86.

765 JACOBUS, L. A. *John Cleveland.* New York: Twayne, 1975.

766 KIMMEY, J. L. "John Cleveland and the Satiric Couplet in the Restoration." *PQ*, 37 (1958), 410−23.

767 KORSHIN, P. J. "The Evolution of Neoclassic Poetics. . . . " See **198**.

768 LEVIN, H. "John Cleveland and the Conceit." *Criterion*, 14 (1934−35), 40−53.

769 WEDGWOOD, C. V. "A Metaphysical Satirist." *The Listener*, 59 (1958), 769−71.

Abraham Cowley (1618– 1667)

Editions

770 *Poetry and Prose*, ed. L. C. Martin. Oxford: Clarendon Press, 1949.

771 *The English Writings*, ed. A. R. Waller. Cambridge: Cambridge University Press, 1905–6.

772 [*Selections*], ed. H. N. Maclean. See **47**.

773 *Selected Poetry and Prose*, ed. J. G. Taaffe. Arlington Heights: AHM Publishing Corp., 1970.

774 *The Mistress, With Other Select Poems*, ed. J. H. A. Sparrow. London: Nonesuch, 1926.

775 *The Civil War*, ed. A. D. Pritchard. Toronto: University of Toronto Press, 1974.

776 *Essays and Other Prose Writings*, ed. A. B. Gough. Oxford: Clarendon Press, 1915.

777 *The Essays*, ed. J. R. Lumby, revised A. Tilley. Cambridge: Cambridge University Press, 1923.

Bibliographies

778 BERRY, L. E., ed. "Abraham Cowley: [Bibliography]." See **4**.

779 SPENCER, T., ed. "Abraham Cowley: [Bibliography]." See **17**.

Studies

780 ALLEN, D. C. "Cowley's Pindar." *MLN*, 63 (1948), 184–85.

781 BRADNER, L. *Musae Anglicanae*. See **151**.

782 ELIOT, T. S. "A Note on Two Odes of Cowley." See **47** and **123**.

783 ELLEDGE, S. "Cowley's Ode 'Of Wit' and Longinus on the Sublime: A Study of One Definition of the Word *Wit*." *MLQ*, 9 (1948), 185–98.

784 GHOSH, J. C. "Abraham Cowley (1618–1667)." *SR*, 61 (1953), 433–47.

785 GOLDSTEIN, H. D. "*Anglorum Pindarus:* Model and Milieu." *CL*, 17 (1965), 299–310.

786 GOLDSTEIN, H. D. "*Discordia Concors*, Decorum and Cowley." *ES*, 49 (1968), 481–89.

787 HINMAN, R. B. " 'Truth is Truest Poesy': The Influence of the New Philosophy on Abraham Cowley." *ELH*, 23 (1956), 194–203.

788 HINMAN, R. B. *Abraham Cowley's World of Order.* Cambridge: Harvard University Press, 1960.

789 JOHNSON, S. "Abraham Cowley." See **47, 193, 878,** and **958.**

790 KORSHIN, P. J. "The Theoretical Bases of Cowley's Later Poetry." *SP,* 66 (1969), 756—76.

791 LARSON, C. "The Somerset-House Poems of Cowley and Waller." *PLL,* 10 (1974), 126—35.

792 LOISEAU, J. *Abraham Cowley's Reputation in England.* Paris: Didier, 1931.

793 MADDISON, C. [Odes]. See **203.**

794 NETHERCOT, A. H. "The Relation of Cowley's Pindarics to Pindar's Odes" *MP,* 19 (1921), 107—9.

795 NETHERCOT, A. H. "The Reputation of Abraham Cowley." *PMLA,* 38 (1923), 588—641.

796 NETHERCOT, A. H. "Abraham Cowley's 'Discourse Concerning Style.' " *RES,* 2 (1926), 385—404.

797 NETHERCOT, A. H. "Abraham Cowley's Essays." *JEGP,* 29 (1930), 114—30.

798 NETHERCOT, A. H. *Abraham Cowley: The Muses's Hannibal.* London: Oxford University Press, 1931; New York: Russell & Russell, 1967.

799 PETTET, E. C. "A Study of Abraham Cowley." *English,* 4 (1943), 86—89.

800 RAM, T. "Cowley and the Epic Poem: The Failure of the *Davideis.*" *Calcutta Review,* NS. 1 (1969), 565—71.

801 RØSTVIG, M. S. "Structural Images in Cowley and Herbert." *ES,* 54 (1973), 121—29.

802 SHAFER, R. "Abraham Cowley." See **237.**

803 TAAFFE, J. G. *Abraham Cowley.* New York: Twayne, 1972.

804 WALLERSTEIN, R. C. "Cowley as a Man of Letters." *Transactions of the Wisconsin Academy of Sciences, Arts, and Letters,* 27 (1932), 127—40.

805 WALTON, G. "Abraham Cowley . . . ." See **255.**

806 WALTON, G. "Abraham Cowley." See **7.**

Richard Crashaw (1612— 1649)

Editions

807 *The Poems, English, Latin and Greek,* ed. L. C. Martin. Oxford, Clarendon Press, 1927; second edition, 1957.

808 *The Complete Poetry,* ed. G. W. Williams. Garden City: Doubleday, 1970; New York: Norton, 1972.

Bibliographies

809 BERRY, L. E., ed. "Richard Crashaw: [Bibliography]." See **4**.

810 SPENCER, T., ed. "Richard Crashaw: [Bibliography]." See **17**.

Studies

811 ADAMS, R. M. "Taste and Bad Taste in Metaphysical Poetry: Richard Crashaw and Dylan Thomas." *HudRev,* 8 (1955), 60—77; and see **196**.

812 ALLISON, A. F. "Some Influences in Crashaw's Poem 'On a Prayer Book Sent to Mrs. M. R.' " *RES,* 23 (1947), 34—42.

813 ALLISON, A. F. "Crashaw and St. François de Sales." *RES,* 24 (1948), 295—302.

814 ANDERSON, J. B. "Richard Crashaw, St. Teresa, and St. John of the Cross." *Discourse,* 10 (1967), 421—28.

815 BENNETT, J. "Richard Crashaw." See **148**.

816 BERTONASCO, M. "A New Look at Crashaw and 'The Weeper.' " *TSLL,* 10 (1968), 177—88.

817 BERTONASCO, M. F. "Crashaw and the Emblem." *ES,* 49 (1969), 530—34.

818 BERTONASCO, M. F. *Crashaw and the Baroque.* University: University of Alabama Press, 1971.

819 CHAMBERS, L. "In Defense of 'The Weeper.' " *PLL,* 3 (1967), 111—21.

820 CIRILLO, A. R. "Crashaw's 'Epiphany Hymn': The Dawn of Christian Time." *SP,* 67 (1970), 67—88.

821 COLLMER, R. G. "Crashaw's 'Death more misticall and high.' " *JEGP,* 55 (1956), 373—80.

822 DOUGHTY, W. L. "Cross and Crucifix: Richard Crashaw." See **164**.

823 ELIOT, T. S. "A Note on Richard Crashaw." *For Lancelot Andrewes.* London: Faber & Gwyer, 1928.

824 FARNHAM, A. E. "Saint Theresa and the Coy Mistress." *BUSE,* 2 (1956), 226—39.

825 HARRISON, R. "Erotic Imagery in Crashaw's 'Musicks Duell,' " *SCN,* 25 (1967), 47—49.

826 HOWARD, T. T. "Herbert and Crashaw: Notes on Meditative Focus." *GorR,* 11 (1968), 79—98.

827 JACOBUS, L. A. "Richard Crashaw as Mannerist." *BuR,* 18, iii (1971), 79—88.

828 LARSON, K. J. [Latin Poetry.] See **150**.

829 LEISHMAN, J. B. "Richard Crashaw." See **201**.

830 MADSEN, W. G. "A Reading of 'Musicks Duell.' " *Studies in Honor of John Wilcox,* ed. A. D. Wallace and W. O. Ross. Detroit: Wayne State University Press, 1958.

831 MANNING, S. "The Meaning of 'The Weeper.' " *ELH*, 22 (1955), 34–47.

832 MARTZ, L. L. "Richard Crashaw: Love's Architecture." See **209.**

833 McCANLES, M. "The Rhetoric of the Sublime in Crashaw's Poetry." See **241.**

834 NEILL, K. "Structure and Symbol in Crashaw's *Hymn in the Nativity.*" *PMLA*, 63 (1948), 101–13.

835 PETER, J. "Crashaw and 'The Weeper.' " *Scrutiny*, 19 (1953), 258–73.

836 PETERSSON, R. T. *The Art of Ecstasy: Teresa, Bernini, and Crashaw.* London: Routledge & Kegan Paul, 1970.

837 PRAZ, M. "The Flaming Heart: Richard Crashaw and the Baroque." See **228.**

838 RASPA, A. "Crashaw and the Jesuit Aesthetic." *UTQ*, 36 (1966–67), 37–54.

839 RICKEY, M. E. *Rhyme and Meaning in Richard Crashaw.* Lexington: University of Kentucky Press, 1961; New York: Haskell House, 1973.

840 SCHAAR, C. *Marino and Crashaw: "Sospetto d'Herode": A Commentary.* Lund: Gleerup, 1971.

841 STRIER, R. "Crashaw's Other Voice." *SEL*, 9 (1969), 135–51.

842 TYTELL, J. "Sexual Imagery in the Secular and Sacred Poems of Richard Crashaw." *L&P*, 21 (1971), 21–27.

843 WALLERSTEIN, R. C. *Richard Crashaw: A Study in Style and Poetic Development.* Madison: University of Wisconsin Press, 1935; New York: Lemma, 1972.

844 WARREN, A. "The Mysticism of Richard Crashaw." *Symposium*, 4 (1933), 135–55.

845 WARREN, A. *Richard Crashaw: A Study in Baroque Sensibility.* Baton Rouge: Louisiana State University Press, 1939; Ann Arbor: University of Michigan Press, 1957.

846 WHITE, H. C. "Richard Crashaw. . . . " See **262.**

847 WILLEY, B. *Richard Crashaw.* Cambridge: Cambridge University Press, 1949.

848 WILLIAMS, G. W. *Image and Symbol in the Sacred Poetry of Richard Crashaw.* Columbia: University of South Carolina Press, 1963.

849 WILLY, M. "Richard Crashaw." See **266.**

William Davenant (1606– 1668)

Editions

850 *The Works* [*1673*]. New York: Benjamin Blom, 1968.

851 *The Shorter Poems, and Songs from the Plays and Masques,* ed. A. M. Gibbs. Oxford: Clarendon Press, 1972.

852 *Selected Poems,* ed. D. Bush. Cambridge: Harvard University Press, 1943.

853 *Gondibert,* ed. D. F. Gladish. Oxford: Clarendon Press, 1971.

Studies

854 GIBBS, A. M. "A Davenant Imitation of Donne?" *RES,* 18 (1967), 45–48.

855 HARBAGE, A. *Sir William Davenant: Poet Venturer.* Philadelphia: University of Pennsylvania Press, 1935.

856 NETHERCOT, A. H. *Sir William D'Avenant: Poet Laureate and Playwright-Manager.* Chicago: University of Chicago Press, 1938; New York: Russell & Russell, 1967.

John Denham (1615– 1669)

Editions

857 *The Poetical Works,* ed. T. H. Banks. New Haven: Yale University Press; London: Oxford University Press, 1928; Hamden: Archon, 1969.

858 *Cooper's Hill,* ed. B. O Hehir. See **866.**

859 [*Selections*], ed. H. N. Maclean. See **47.**

Studies

860 AUBIN, R. "Materials for a Study of the Influence of *Cooper's Hill.*" *ELH,* 1 (1934), 198–204.

861 BANKS, T. H. "Sir John Denham's *Cooper's Hill.*" *MLR,* 21 (1926), 269–77.

862 JOHNSON, S. "John Denham." See **47** and **193.**

863 KORSHIN, P. J. "The Evolution of Neoclassic Poetics. . . . " See **198.**

864 O HEHIR, B. "Vergil's First *Georgic* and Denham's *Cooper's Hill.*" *PQ,* 42 (1963), 542–47.

865 O HEHIR, B. *Harmony from Discords: A Life of Sir John Denham.* Berkeley: University of California Press, 1968.

866 O HEHIR, B. *Expans'd Hieroglyphicks: A Study of Sir John Denham's "Cooper's Hill" with a Critical Edition of the Poem.* Berkeley: University of California Press, 1969.

867 PUTNEY, R. "The View from Cooper's Hill." *UCSLL,* 6 (1957), 13–22.

868 WALLERSTEIN, R. "The Development of the Rhetoric and Metre of the Heroic Couplet. . . ." See **253**.

869 WASSERMAN, E. R. "Denham: *Cooper's Hill.*" *The Subtler Language: Critical Readings of Neoclassic and Romantic Poems.* Baltimore: Johns Hopkins Press, 1959; and see **47**.

John Donne (1572— 1631)

Editions

870 *The Complete Poems,* ed. R. E. Bennett. Chicago: Packard, 1942; New York: Hendricks House, 1958.

871 *The Poems;* Vol. I: *The Text of the Poems with Appendixes;* Vol. II: *Introduction and Commentary;* ed. H. J. C. Grierson. Oxford: Clarendon Press; New York: Oxford University Press, 1912, etc.

872 *The Poems,* ed. H. J. C. Grierson. New York: Oxford University Press, 1929.

873 *The Complete Poetry,* ed. J. T. Shawcross. New York: New York University Press; Garden City: Doubleday, 1967.

874 *The Complete English Poems,* ed. A. J. Smith. Harmondsworth: Penguin, 1971; New York: St. Martin's, 1974.

875 *Poems,* ed. H. L. Fausset. London: Dent, 1931.

876 *The Poems,* ed. F. Kermode, New York: Heritage, 1970.

877 *Selected Poetry,* ed. M. Bewley. New York: New American Library, 1966.

878 *Poetry,* selected and ed. A. L. Clements. New York: Norton, 1966.

879 *A Selection of His Poetry,* ed. J. Hayward. Baltimore: Penguin, 1950.

880 *Selected Poems,* ed. J. Reeves. London: Heinemann; New York: Macmillan, 1958.

881 *Selected Poems,* ed. M. A. Shaaber. Arlington Heights Ill.: AHM Publishing Corp., 1958.

882 [Selected Poems], ed. A. Wanning. New York: Dell, 1962.

883 *Complege Poetry and Selected Prose,* ed. C. M. Coffin. New York: Modern Library, 1952.

884 *Poetry and Prose,* ed. W. H. Garrod. Oxford: Clarendon Press, 1946.

885 *Complete Poetry and Selected Prose,* ed. J. Hayward. Bloomsbury: Nonesuch; New York: Random House, 1929, etc.

886 *Poetry and Prose,* ed. F. J. Warnke. New York: Modern Library, 1967.

887 *The Anniversaries,* ed. F. Manley. Baltimore: Johns Hopkins Press, 1963.

888 *The Divine Poems,* ed. H. Gardner. Oxford: Clarendon Press; New York: Oxford University Press, 1952.

889 *The Elegies and The Songs and Sonnets,* ed. H. Gardner. Oxford: Clarendon Press; New York: Oxford University Press, 1965.

890 *The Satires, Epigrams, and Verse Letters,* ed. W. Milgate. Oxford: Clarendon Press; New York: Oxford University Press, 1967.

891 *The Songs and Sonets,* ed. T. Redpath. London: Methuen, 1956.

892 *Shorter Prose Works,* ed. E. Simpson and R. E. Bennett. New York: Farrar, Straus, 1948.

893 *Select Prose,* chosen by E. Simpson, ed. H. Gardner and T. Healy. Oxford: Clarendon Press; New York: Oxford University Press, 1967.

894 *The Courtier's Library,* ed. E. M. Simpson. London: Nonesuch, 1930.

895 *Biathanatos: Reproduced from the First Edition,* ed. J. W. Hebel. New York: Facsimile Text Society, 1930.

896 *Devotions Upon Emergent Occasions, Together with Death's Duel.* Ann Arbor: University of Michigan Press, 1959.

897 *Devotions upon Emergent Occasions,* ed. W. H. Draper. Boston: Small, Maynard, 1962.

898 *Devotions upon Emergent Occasions,* ed. J. Sparrow. Cambridge: Cambridge University Press, 1923.

899 *Essays in Divinity,* ed. E. M. Simpson. Oxford: Clarendon Press; New York: Oxford University Press, 1952.

900 *Ignatius' His Conclave,* ed. C. M. Coffin. New York: Facsimile Text Society, 1941.

901 *Ignatius His Conclave,* ed. T. S. Healy. New York: Oxford University Press, 1970.

902 *Ivvenilia: or, Certain Paradoxes and Problems,* ed. R. E. Bennett. New York: Facsimile Text Society, 1936.

903 *Paradoxes and Problems . . . , with Two Characters and an Essay of Valour.* Soho: Nonesuch, 1923.

904 *The Prayers,* ed. H. H. Umbach. New York: Twayne, 1951.

905 *The Sermons,* ed. G. R. Potter and E. M. Simpson, 10 vols. Berkeley: University of California Press, 1953−62.

906 *Sermons: Selected . . . ,* ed. T. A. Gill. New York: Meridian, 1958.

907 *Prebend Sermons,* ed. J. M. Mueller. Cambridge: Harvard University Press, 1971.

908 *Sermons on the Psalms and Gospels, with a Selection of Prayers and Meditations,* ed. E. M. Simpson. Berkeley: University of California Press; London: Cambridge University Press, 1963.

909 *The Showing Forth of Christ: Sermons . . . ,* selected and ed. E. Fuller. New York: Harper & Row, 1964.

910 *Sermons: Selected Passages,* ed. L. P. Smith. Oxford: Clarendon Press; New York: Oxford University Press, 1919.

911 *Deaths Duell: A Sermon delivered before King Charles I . . . ,* ed. G. Keynes. Brookline: Godine; London: Bodley Head, 1973.

Bibliographies and Concordance

912 BERRY, L. E., ed. "John Donne: [Bibliography]." See **4**.

913 COMBS, H. C., and Z. R. A. SULLENS, eds. *A Concordance to the English Poems of John Donne*. Chicago: Packard, 1940.

914 KEYNES, G., ed. *A Bibliography of the Works of Dr. John Donne*. . . . Cambridge: Baskerville Club, 1914; third edition, Cambridge: Cambridge University Press, 1958; Oxford: Clarendon Press, 1973.

915 MILGATE, W., ed. "Donne, 1572 – 1631." See **6**.

916 ROBERTS, J. R., ed. *John Donne: An Annotated Bibliography of Modern Criticism, 1912 – 1967*. Columbia: University of Missouri Press, 1973.

917 SPENCER, T., ed. "John Donne: [Bibliography]." See **17**.

918 WHITE, W., ed. *John Donne: A Bibliography of Periodical Articles*. Boston: Faxon, 1942.

919 WHITE, W. "Sir Geoffrey Keynes's Bibliography of John Donne: A Review with Addenda." *Bulletin of Bibliography*, 22 (1959), 186 – 89.

Comprehensive Studies

920 ANDREASEN, N. J. C. *John Donne: Conservative Revolutionary*. Princeton: Princeton University Press, 1967.

921 BAKER-SMITH, D. "*John Donne's Critique of True Religion*. See **996**.

922 BALD, R. C. *Donne and the Drurys*. Cambridge: Cambridge University Press, 1959.

923 BALD, R. C. *John Donne: A Life*, ed. W. Milgate. New York: Oxford University Press, 1970.

924 BATTENHOUSE, R. W. "The Grounds of Religious Toleration in the Thought of John Donne." *CH*, 11 (1942), 217 – 48.

925 BENHAM, A. R. "The Myth of John Donne the Rake." *Renaissance Studies in Honor of Hardin Craig*, ed. B. Maxwell et al. Stanford: Stanford University Press, 1941; Folcroft: Folcroft Library Editions, 1972.

926 BENNETT, J. "John Donne: . . . Technical Originality." See **148**.

927 BEWLEY, M. "Religious Cynicism in Donne's Poetry." *KR*, 14 (1952), 619 – 46.

928 BLANCHARD, M. M. "The Leap into Darkness: Donne, Herbert, and God." *Ren*, 17 (1964), 38 – 50.

929 BREDVOLD, L. I. "The Naturalism of Donne in Relation to Some Renaissance Traditions." *JEGP*, 22 (1923), 471 – 502; and see **958**.

930 BREDVOLD, L. I. "The Religious Thought of Donne in Relation to Medieval and Later Traditions." *Studies in Shakespeare, Milton, and Donne*. New York: Macmillan, 1925; New York: Haskell House, 1964.

931 BULLOUGH, G. "Donne: The Man of Law." See **943**.

932 CAROLINE, Sr. M. "The Existentialist Attitude of John Donne." *XUS*, 7, i (1968), 37–50.

933 CATHCART, D. *Doubting Conscience: Donne and the Poetry of Moral Argument.* Ann Arbor: University of Michigan Press, 1974.

934 CLIVE, M. *Jack and the Doctor:* [*A Life*]. New York: St. Martin's, 1966.

935 COFFIN, C. M. *John Donne and the New Philosophy.* New York: Columbia University Press, 1937; New York: Humanities Press, 1958.

936 COFFIN, C. M. "Donne's Divinity." *KR,* 16 (1954), 292–98.

937 COLIE, R. L. "John Donne and the Paradoxes of Incarnation." See **79**.

938 COX, R. G. "The Poems of John Donne." See **7**.

939 CROFTS, J. E. V. "John Donne: A Reconsideration." See **944**.

940 DOUDS, J. B. "Donne's Technique of Dissonance." *PMLA,* 52 (1937), 1051–61.

941 ELIOT, T. S. "The Metaphysical Poets." See **86**.

942 EMPSON, W. "Rescuing Donne." See **943**.

943 FIORE, P. A., ed. *Just So Much Honor: Essays Commemorating the Four-Hundredth Anniversary of the Birth of John Donne.* University Park: Pennsylvania State University Press, 1972.

944 GARDNER, H., ed. *John Donne: A Collection of Critical Essays.* Englewood Cliffs: Prentice-Hall, 1962.

945 GERALDINE, Sr. M. "John Donne and the Mindes Indeavours." *SEL,* 5 (1965), 115–32.

946 GOHN, E. S. "Dating Donne and Scholarly Sentimentality." *PMASAL,* 48 (1963), 609–19.

947 GRANSDEN, K. W. *John Donne.* London, New York: Longmans, Green, 1954; revised edition, Hamden: Shoestring Press, 1969.

948 GRIERSON, H. J. C. "John Donne and the Via Media." *MLR,* 43 (1948), 305–14. *Criticism and Creation.* London: Chatto & Windus, 1949.

949 GUSS, D. L. *John Donne, Petrarchist: Italianate Conceits and Love Theory in the Songs and Sonets.* Detroit: Wayne State University Press, 1966.

950 HENRICKSEN, B. "Donne's Orthodoxy." *TSLL,* 14 (1972), 5–16.

951 HICKEY, R. L. "Donne's Art of Memory." *TSL,* 3 (1958), 29–36.

952 HUGHES, R. E. *The Porogress of the Soul: The Interior Career of John Donne.* New York: Morrow, 1968.

953 HUNT, C. *Donne's Poetry: Essays in Literary Analysis.* New Haven: Yale University Press, 1954; Hamden: Shoestring Press, 1969.

954 HUSAIN, I. *The Dogmatic and Mystical Theology of John Donne.* London: Society for Promoting Christian Knowledge; New York: Macmillan, 1938; Folcraft: Folcraft Press, 1969.

955 JACKSON, R. S. *John Donne's Christian Vocation.* Evanston: Northwestern University Press, 1970.

956 JOHNSON, S. "Abraham Cowley." See **47, 193, 878,** and **957**.

957 KERMODE, F. *John Donne.* London: Longmans, 1957; revised edition, 1961.

958 KERMODE, F., ed. *Discussions of Donne.* Boston: Heath, 1962.

959 KERRIGAN, W. "The Fearful Accommodations of John Donne." *ELR,* 4 (1974), 337–63.

960 KREMIN, K. R. *The Imagination of Resurrection: The Poetic Continuity of a Religious Motif in Donne, Blake, and Yeats.* Lewisburg: Bucknell University Press, 1972.

961 LE COMTE, E. S. *Grace to a Witty Sinner: A Life of Donne.* New York: Walker, 1965.

962 LE COMTE, E. S. "Jack Donne: From Rake to Husband." See **943.**

963 LEISHMAN, J. B. "John Donne." See **201.**

964 LEISHMAN, J. B. *The Monarch of Wit: An Analytical and Comparative Study of the Poetry of John Donne.* London: Hutchinson, 1951, etc.

965 LOUTHAN, D. *The Poetry of John Donne: A Study in Explication.* New York: Twayne, 1951.

966 MAHOOD, M. M. "Donne: The Progress of the Soul." See **204.**

967 MARTZ, L. L. "Donne and the Meditative Tradition." *Thought,* 34 (1959), 269–78; and see **210.**

968 MARTZ, L. L. "John Donne: The Meditative Voice." *MR,* 1 (1960), 326–42; and see **210.**

969 MILES, J. *Poetry and Change: Donne, Milton, Wordsworth and the Equilibrium of the Present.* Berkeley: University of California Press, 1974.

970 MILES, J. "Ifs, Ands, Buts for the Reader of Donne." See **943.**

971 MOLONEY, M. F. *John Donne: His Flight from Mediaevalism.* Urbana: University of Illinois Press, 1944.

972 MOLONEY, M. F. "John Donne and the Jesuits." *MLQ,* 8 (1947), 426–29.

973 MOLONEY, M. F. "Donne's Metrical Practice." *PMLA,* 65 (1950), 232–39.

974 NELLY, V. *The Poet Donne: A Study in his Dialectical Method.* Dublin: Cork University Press, 1969.

975 NYE, R. "The Body is his Book: The Poetry of John Donne." *CritQ,* 14 (1972), 345–60.

976 PARTRIDGE, A. C. *The Language of Renaissance Poetry:* [. . . *Donne*]. London: Deutsch, 1971.

977 POTTER, G. R. "John Donne: Poet to Priest." *University of California Publications: English Series,* 10 (1954), 105–26.

978 POWER, H. W. "The Speaker as Creator: The Voice in Donne's Poems." *XUS,* 11, i (1972), 21–28.

979 PRAZ, M. *John Donne.* Torino: S.A.I.E., 1958.

980 PRAZ, M. "Donne's Relation to the Poetry of His Time." See **17, 228,** and **944.**

981 PRAZ, M. "Baroque in England." *MP,* 61 (1964), 169–79.

982 QUINN, D. "Donne and the Wane of Wonder." *ELH,* 36 (1969), 626–47.

983 RAMSAY, M. P. *Les doctrines Médiévales chez Donne.* New York: Oxford University Press, 1917.

984 ROBERTS, D. A. "The Death Wish of John Donne." *PMLA*, 62 (1947), 958–76.

985 ROSTON, M. *The Soul of Wit: A Study of John Donne.* Oxford: Clarendon Press, 1974.

986 ROWE, F. A. *I Launch at Paradise: A Consideration of John Donne, Poet and Preacher.* London: Epworth Press, 1964.

987 RUGOFF, M. A. *Donne's Imagery; A Study in Creative Sources.* New York: Corporate Press, 1939; New York: Russell & Russell, 1962.

988 SACTON, A. "Donne and the Privacy of Verse." *SEL*, 7 (1967), 67–82.

989 SANDERS, W. *John Donne's Poetry.* Cambridge: Cambridge University Press, 1971.

990 SICHERMAN, C. M. "The Mocking Voices of Donne and Marvell." *BuR*, 17, ii (1969), 32–46.

991 SICHERMAN, C. M. "Donne's Discoveries." *SEL*, 11 (1971), 69–88.

992 SIMONS, I. *Some Problems of Donne Criticism.* Brussels: Didier, 1952.

993 SKELTON, R. "The Poetry of John Donne." *Stratford-upon-Avon Studies*, 2 (1960), 203–20.

994 SLOAN, T. O. "The Rhetoric in the Poetry of John Donne." *SEL*, 3 (1963), 31–44.

995 SMITH, A. J. "Sources of Difficulty and of Value in the Poetry of John Donne." *LM*, 7 (1957), 182–90.

996 SMITH, A. J., ed. *John Donne: Essays in Celebration.* London: Methuen, 1972; New York: Barnes & Noble, 1973.

997 SPENCER, T., ed. *A Garland for John Donne.* Cambridge: Harvard University Press, 1931; Gloucester: Peter Smith, 1958.

998 SPROTT, S. E. "The Legend of Jack Donne the Libertine." *UTQ*, 19 (1949–50), 335–53.

999 STAMPFER, J. *John Donne and the Metaphysical Gesture.* New York: Funk & Wagnals, 1970.

1000 STEIN, A. "Structures of Sound in Donne's Verse." *KR*, 13 (1951), 20–36, 256–78.

1001 STEIN, A. *John Donne's Lyrics: The Eloquence of Action.* Minneapolis: University of Minnesota Press, 1962.

1002 THOMSON, P. "John Donne and the Countess of Bedford." *MLR*, 44 (1949), 329–40.

1003 ULREY, P. "The 'One' in Donne's Poetry." *RenP* (1961; for 1958–60), 76–83.

1004 UNGER, L. *Donne's Poetry and Modern Criticism.* Chicago: Regnery, 1950.

1005 WALLER, G. F. "John Donne's Changing Attitudes to Time." *SEL*, 14 (1974), 79–89.

1006 WALTON, I. "The Life of Dr. John Donne." See **2332, 2340–43.**

1007 WARREN, A. "The Very Reverend Dr. Donne." *KR*, 16 (1954), 268–77.

1008 WHITE, H. C. ". . . John Donne." See **262.**

1009 WHITE, H. C. "John Donne and the Psychology of Spiritual Effort." See **101.**

1010 WHITLOCK, B. W. "Donne's University Years." *ES*, 43 (1962), 1 – 20.

1011 WIGGINS, E. L. "Logic in the Poetry of John Donne." *SP*, 42 (1945), 41 – 60.

1012 WILLIAMSON, G. "John Donne and his Shroud." See **263.**

1013 WILLIAMSON, G. "The Libertine Donne." *PQ*, 13 (1934), 276 – 91; and see **138.**

1014 WILLIAMSON, G. "The Two Worlds of John Donne." See **265.**

1015 WILSON, G. R., Jr. "The Interplay of Perception and Reflection: Mirror Imagery in Donne's Poetry." *SEL*, 9 (1969), 107 – 21.

1016 WINNY, J. *A Preface to Donne.* London: Longmans, 1970.

1017 WOODHOUSE, A. S. P. "The Seventeenth Century: Donne and His Successors." *The Poet and His Faith* . . . . Chicago: University of Chicago Press, 1966.

Studies of Topics

1018 ADAMS, R. M. "Donne and Eliot: Metaphysicals." *KR*, 16 (1954), 278 – 91.

1019 ALLEN, D. C. "John Donne's Knowledge of Renaissance Medicine." *JEGP*, 42 (1943), 322 – 42.

1020 ALLEN, D. C. "Donne's Specular Stone." *MLN*, 61 (1946), 63 – 64.

1021 ALLEN, D. C. "The Genesis of Donne's Dreams." *MLN*, 75 (1960), 293 – 95.

1022 ALLEN, D. C. "Donne and the Ship Metaphor." *MLN*, 76 (1961), 308 – 12.

1023 BALD, R. C. *Donne's Influence in English Literature.* Morpeth: St. John's College Press, 1932; Gloucester: Peter Smith, 1965.

1024 BOZANICH, R. "Donne and Ecclesiastes." *PMLA*, 90 (1975), 270 – 76.

1025 BRADBROOK, F. W. "John Donne and Ben Jonson." *N&Q*, 4 (1957), 146 – 47.

1026 BRYAN, R. A. "John Donne's Use of the Anathema." *JEGP*, 61 (1962), 305 – 12.

1027 CRASHAW, E. "Hermetic Elements in Donne's Poetic Vision." See **996.**

1028 DUNCAN, E. H. "Donne's Alchemical Figures." *ELH*, 9 (1942), 262 – 84; and see **958.**

1029 DURAND, L. G. "Sponde and Donne: Lens and Prism." *CL*, 21 (1969), 319 – 36.

1030 ELIOT, T. S. "Donne in Our Time." See **997.**

1031 GARDNER, H. "The Titles of Donne's Poems." *Friendships Garland: Essays Presented to Mario Praz.* . . . Roma: Edizioni di Storia e Letteratura, 1966.

1032 GUSS, D. L. "Donne's Conceits and Petrarchan Wit." *PMLA*, 78 (1963), 307 – 14.

1033 GUSS, D. L. "Donne's Petrarchism." *JEGP*, 64 (1965), 17 – 28.

1034 HARRIS, V. "John Donne and the Theatre." *PQ*, 41 (1962), 257 – 69.

1035 KLAMMER, E. "Cosmography in Donne's Poetry." *Cresset,* 32, i (1968), 14—15.

1036 LEAVIS, F. R. "The Influence of Donne on Modern Poetry." *The Bookman,* 79 (1931), 346—47.

1037 LEDERER, J. "John Donne and Emblematic Practice." *RES,* 22 (1946), 182—200.

1038 LEWALSKI, B. K. "Donne's Poetry of Compliment: The Speaker's Stance and the Topoi of Praise." See **114.**

1039 MALLOCH, A. E. "John Donne and the Casuists." *SEL,* 2 (1962), 57—76.

1040 MAZZEO, J. A. "Notes on John Donne's Alchemical Imagery." *Isis,* 48 (1957), 103—23; and see **110.**

1041 McCANLES, M. "Paradox in Donne." *SRen,* 13 (1966), 266—87.

1042 MILLS, L. L. "The Literary Character of Donne's References to Specular Stone." *HAB,* 1 (1972), 37—21.

1043 MORRIS, B. " 'Not, Siren-like, to Tempt': Donne and the Composers." See **996.**

1044 MURRAY, W. A. "Donne and Paracelsus: An Essay in Interpretation." *RES,* 25 (1949), 115—23.

1045 ORNSTEIN, R. "Donne, Montaigne, and Natural Law." *JEGP,* 55 (1956), 213—29.

1046 PARISH, J. E. "Donne as a Petrarchan." *N&Q,* 4 (1957), 377—78.

1047 RINGLER, R. N. "Donne's Specular Stone." *MLR,* 60 (1965), 333—39.

1048 SHARROCK, R. "Wit, Passion, and Ideal Love: Reflections on the Cycle of Donne's Reputation." See **943.**

1049 SMITH, A. J. "Donne's Reputation." See **996.**

1050 SMITH, A. J. "The Dismissal of Love; Or, Was Donne a Neoplatonic Lover?" See **996.**

1051 STEIN, A. "Donne's Prosody." *PMLA,* 59 (1944), 373—97.

1052 STEIN, A. "Donne and the Satiric Spirit." *ELH,* 11 (1944), 266—82.

1053 STEIN, A. "Donne's Obscurity and the Elizabethan Tradition." *ELH,* 13 (1946), 98—118.

1054 STEIN, A. "Donne and the 1920's: A Problem in Historical Consciousness." *ELH,* 27 (1960), 16—29.

1055 TILLOTSON, K. "Donne's Poetry in the Nineteenth Century." See **84.**

1056 TOMLINSON, T. B. "Donne and His Critics." *CR,* 13 (1970), 84—100.

1057 WENDELL, J. P. "Two Cruxes in the Poetry of Donne." *MLN,* 63 (1948), 477—81.

1058 WILLIAMSON, G. "Donne and the Poetry of Today." See **997.**

1059 WILLY, M. "The Poetry of Donne: Its Interest and Influence Today." *E&S,* 7 (1954), 78—104.

Studies: Poems

Songs and Sonnets

1060 AHRENDS, G. "Discordia concors: John Donne's 'Nocturnal Upon S. Lucies Day.' " *NS*, 20 (1971), 68–85.

1061 ALLEN, D. C. "Donne's Compass Figure." *MLN*, 71 (1956), 256–57.

1062 ALLEN, D. C. "Donne on the Mandrake." *MLN*, 74 (1959), 393–97.

1063 BAUER, R. J. "The Great Prince in Donne's 'The Extasie.' " *TSL*, 14 (1969), 93–102.

1064 BENNETT, J. "The Love Poetry of John Donne: A Reply to Mr. C. S. Lewis." See **123, 196,** and **878.**

1065 BROOKS, C. "The Language of Paradox: 'The Canonization.' " *The Well Wrought Urn.* New York: Reynal & Hitchcock, 1947; New York: Harcourt, Brace, 1956; and see **878, 944,** and **958.**

1066 BRUMBLE, H. D., III. "John Donne's 'The Flea': Some Implications of the Encyclopedic and Poetic Flea Traditions." *CritQ*, 15 (1973), 147–54.

1067 CAREY, J. "Notes on Two of Donne's *Songs and Sonnets:* [A Valediction: 'Of Weeping' and 'The Extasie']." *RES*, 16 (1965), 50–53.

1068 CHAMBERS, A. B. "The Fly in Donne's 'Canonization.' *JEGP*, 65 (1966), 252–59.

1069 CLAIR, J. A. "Donne's 'The Canonization.' " *PMLA*, 80 (1965), 300–302.

1070 COLLINS, C. "Donne's *The Canonization.*" *Expl*, 12 (1953), Item 3.

1071 CORIN, F. "A Note on Donne's 'Canonization.' " *ES*, 50 (1969), 89–93.

1072 CROSS, K. G. " 'Balm' in Donne and Shakespeare: Ironic Intention in *The Extasie.*" *MLN*, 71 (1956), 480–82.

1073 CRUTWELL, P. "The Love Poetry of John Donne: Pedantique Weedes or Fresh Invention?" *Stratford-upon-Avon Studies*, 11 (1970), 11–40.

1074 DAICHES, D. "A Reading of the 'Good-Morrow.' " See **943.**

1075 DIVINE, J. D. "Compass and Circle in Donne's 'A Valediction: Forbidding Mourning.' " *PLL*, 9 (1973), 78–80.

1076 DURR, R. A. "Donne's 'The Primrose.' " *JEGP*, 59 (1960), 218–22; and see **878.**

1077 EMPSON, W. " 'A Valediction: Of Weeping.' " See **171** and **944.**

1078 FLEISSNER, R. F. "Donne and Dante: The Compass Figure Reinterpreted." *MLN*, 76 (1961), 315–20.

1079 FRECCERO, J. "Donne's 'Valediction Forbidding Mourning.' " *ELH*, 30 (1963), 335–76.

1080 GALLANT, G., and A. L. CLEMENTS. "Harmonized Voices in Donne's 'Songs and Sonets': 'The Dampe.' " *SEL*, 15 (1975), 71–82.

1081 GARDNER, H. "The Argument about 'The Ecstasy.' " See **84.**

1082 GÉRARD, A. "Mannerism and the Scholastic Structure of Donne's 'Extasie.' " *Pubs. de l'Univ. de l'Etat á Elisabeth — Elisabethville*, 1 (1961), 27–37.

1083 GRAZIANI, R. "John Donne's 'The Extasie' and Ecstasy." *RES*, 19 (1968), 121—36.

1084 GRIERSON, H. J. C. "Donne's Love Poetry." See **871** and **944**.

1085 HARDY, B. "Thinking and Feeling in the Songs and Sonnets." See **996**.

1086 HOLLANDER, J. "Donne and the Limits of Lyric." See **996**.

1087 HUGHES, M. Y. "The Lineage of 'The Ecstasie.' " *MLR*, 27 (1932), 1—5.

1088 HUGHES, M. Y. "Some of Donne's Ecstasies." *PMLA*, 75 (1960), 509—18.

1089 HUGHES, R. E. "John Donne's 'Nocturnall Upon S. Lucies Day': A Suggested Resolution." *Cithara*, 4, ii (1965), 60—68.

1090 JOHNSON, B. "Classical Allusions in the Poetry of Donne." *PMLA*, 43 (1928), 1098—1109.

1091 KEEBLE, N. H. "The Love Poetry of John Donne." *Lang&L*, 1, iii (1972), 7—19.

1092 KILEY, F. "A Larger Reading of Donne's 'A Lecture Upon the Shadow.' " *CEA*, 30, vii (1968), 16—17.

1093 LABRIOLA, A. C. "Donne's 'The Canonization': Its Theological Context and its Religious Imagery." *HLQ*, 36 (1973), 327—39.

1094 LAWNICZAK, D. A. "Donne's Sainted Lovers — Again." *Serif*, 6, i (1969), 12—19.

1095 LEGOUIS, P. *Donne the Craftsman: An Essay upon the Structure of the Songs and Sonets.* Paris: Didier, 1928; New York: Russell & Russell, 1962.

1096 LEVINE, G. R. "Satiric Intent and Baroque Design in Donne's 'Go and Catch a Falling Star.' " *NS*, 20 (1971), 384—87.

1097 LEVINE, J. A. " 'The Dissolution': Donne's Twofold Elegy." *ELH*, 28 (1961), 301—15.

1098 LEWALSKI, B. K. "A Donnean Perspective on 'The Exstasie.' " *ELN*, 10 (1973), 258—62.

1099 LEWIS, C. S. "Donne and Love Poetry in the Seventeenth Century." See **123, 196, 878,** and **944**.

1100 LOVELOCK, J., ed. *Donne: Songs and Sonets; A Casebook.* London: Macmillan, 1973.

1101 MAROTTI, A. F. "Donne and 'The Extasie.' " See **241**.

1102 MARTZ, L. L. "John Donne: Love's Philosophy." See **209**.

1103 McCANLES, M. "Distinguish in Order to Unite: Donne's 'The Extasie.' " *SEL*, 6 (1966), 59—75.

1104 McCANN, E. "Donne and Saint Teresa on the Ecstasy." *HLQ*, 17 (1954), 125—32.

1105 McLAUGHLIN, E. " 'The Extasie'—Deceptive or Authentic?" *BuR*, 18, iii (1971), 55—78.

1106 MILGATE, W. " 'Aire and Angles' and the Discrimination of Experience." See **943**.

1107 MILLER, C. H. "Donne's 'A Nocturnal upon S. Lucies Day' and the Nocturns of Matins." *SEL*, 6 (1966), 77—87.

1108 MITCHELL, C. "Donne's 'The Extasie': Love's Sublime Knot." *SEL,* 8 (1968), 91 – 101.

1109 MORILLO, M. "Donne's Compasses: Circles and Right Lines." *ELN,* 3 (1966), 173 – 76.

1110 MURRAY, W. A. "Donne's Gold-Leaf and His Compasses." *MLN,* 73 (1958), 329 – 30.

1111 NOVARR, D. " 'The Extasie': Donne's Address on the States of Union." See **943.**

1112 PARISH, J. E. "The Parley in 'The Extasie.' " *XUS,* 4 (1965), 188 – 92.

1113 POTTER, G. R. "Donne's 'Exstasie': Contra Legouis." *PQ,* 15 (1936), 247 – 53.

1114 POWERS, D. C. "Donne's Compass." *RES,* 9 (1958), 173 – 75.

1115 ROCKETT, W. "Donne's Libertine Rhetoric." *ES,* 52 (1971), 507 – 18.

1116 ROONEY, W. J. " 'The Canonization': The Language of Paradox Reconsidered." *ELH,* 23 (1956), 36 – 47.

1117 RUFFO-FIORE, S. "Donne's 'Parody' of the Petrarchan Lady." *CLS,* 9 (1972), 392 – 406.

1118 RUFFO-FIORE, S. "The Unwanted Heart in Petrarch and Donne." *CL,* 24 (1972), 319 – 27.

1119 SCHAAR, C. " 'Balme' in Donne's 'Exstasie.' " *ES,* 53 (1972), 224 – 25.

1120 SERIG, P. J. "Donne's Compass Image." *N&Q,* 5 (1958), 214 – 15.

1121 SLEIGHT, R. "John Donne: 'A Nocturnall upon S. Lucies Day.' " *Interpretations: Essays on Twelve English Poems,* ed. J. Waine. London, Boston: Routledge & Kegan Paul, 1956, 1972.

1122 SLOAN, T. O. "A Rhetorical Analysis of John Donne's 'The Prohibition.' " *QJS,* 48 (1962), 38 – 45.

1123 SMITH, A. J. "Donne in his Time: A Reading of *The Extasie.*" *RLMC,* 10 (1957), 260 – 75.

1124 SMITH, A. J. "The Metaphysic of Love." *RES,* 9 (1958), 362 – 75; and see **958.**

1125 SMITH, A. J. "New Bearings in Donne: 'Aire and Angeles.' " *English,* 13 (1960), 49 – 53; and see **944.**

1126 SMITH, A. J. *The Songs and Sonets.* London: Arnold; Great Neck: Barron's, 1964.

1127 STEWART, J. F. "Irony in Donne's 'The Funeral.' " *Discourse,* 12 (1969), 193 – 99.

1128 STEWART, J. F. "Image and Idea in Donne's 'The Good-Morrow.' " *Discourse,* 12 (1969), 465 – 76.

1129 TATE, A. "The Point of Dying: Donne's 'Virtuous Men.' " *SR,* 61 (1953), 76 – 81.

1130 TRACI, P. "The Supposed New Rhetoric of Donne's *Songs and Sonets.*" *Discourse,* 11 (1968), 98 – 107.

1131 VICKERS, B. "The 'Songs and Sonnets' and the Rhetoric of Hyperbole." See **996.**

1132 WARREN, A. "Donne's 'Extasie.' " *SP*, 55 (1958), 472 – 80.

1133 WILLIAMSON, G. "The Convention of *The Extasie.*" See **138** and **196.**

Elegies

1134 BOWERS, F. "An Interpretation of Donne's Tenth Elegy." *MLN*, 54 (1939), 280 – 82.

1135 DOEBLER, B. A. "Donne's Incarnate Venus." *SAQ*, 71 (1972), 504 – 12.

1136 DUNCAN-JONES, E. E. "Donne's Praise of Autumnal Beauty: Greek Sources." *MLR*, 56 (1961), 213 – 15.

1137 GILL, R. "*Musa Iocosa Mea:* Thoughts on the Elegies." See **996.**

1138 GREGORY, E. R., Jr. "The Balance of Parts: Imagistic Unity in Donne's 'Elegie XIX.' " *UR*, 35 (1968), 51 – 54.

1139 HUNT, C. "Elegy 19: 'To His Mistress Going to Bed.' " See **878** and **953.**

1140 JACOBSEN, E. "Donne's Elegy VII." *ES*, 45 (1964), Supp., 190 – 96.

1141 LaBRANCHE, A. "*Blanda Elegeia:* The Background to Donne's Elegies." *MLR*, 61 (1966), 357 – 68.

1142 LOVE, H. "Donne's 'To His Mistress Going to Bed.' " *Expl*, 26 (1967), Item 33.

1143 MAIN, W. W. "Donne's *Elegie XIX: Going to Bed.*" *Expl*, 10 (1951), Item 14.

1144 ROCKETT, W. "John Donne: The Ethical Argument of *Elegy III.*" *SEL*, 15 (1975) 57 – 69.

Satires

1145 ANDREASEN, N. D. K. Jr., "Theme and Structure in Donne's Satires." *SEL*, 3 (1963), 59 – 75.

1146 BROSS, A. C. "Alexander Pope's Revisions of John Donne's *Satyres.*" *XUS*, 5 (1966), 133 – 52.

1147 ERSKINE-HILL, H. "Courtiers of Horace: Donne's *Satyre IV;* and Pope's *Fourth Satire of Dr. John Donne. . . .* " See **996.**

1148 GERALDINE, Sr. M. "Donne's *Notitia:* The Evidence of the Satires." *UTQ*, 36 (1966 – 67), 24 – 36.

1149 HUTCHISON, A. N. "Constant Company: John Donne and His Satiric Personae." *Discourse,* 13 (1970), 354 – 63.

1150 JOHNSON, S. F. "Donne's *Satires,* I." *Expl*, 11 (1953), Item 53.

1151 KORTE, D. M. "John Donne's 'Satyres' and a Matter of Rhetoric." *HAB*, 20, iii (1969), 78 – 81.

1152 MOORE, T. V. "Donne's Use of Uncertainty as a Vital Force in *Satyre III.*" *MP*, 67 (1969), 41 – 49.

1153 SHAWCROSS, J. T. "All Attest His Writs Canonical: The Texts, Meaning, and Evaluation of Donne's Satires." See **943.**

1154 SLIGHTS, C. " 'To Stand Inquiring Right': The Casuistry of Donne's 'Satire III.' " *SEL*, 12 (1972), 85 – 101.

1155 SLOAN, T. O. "The Persona as Rhetor: An Interpretation of Donne's *Satyre III.*" *QJS*, 51 (1965), 14–27.

1156 SMITH, H. *Elizabethan Poetry: A Study in Conventions.* Cambridge: Harvard University Press, 1952; Ann Arbor: University of Michigan Press, 1968.

1157 WILLIAMSON, G. "Donne's Satirical *Progresse of the Soule.*" *ELH*, 36 (1969), 250–64.

1158 ZIVLEY, S. "Imagery in John Donne's *Satyres.*" *SEL*, 6 (1966), 87–95.

Epistles and Epithalamia

1159 BALD, R. C. "Donne's Early Verse Letters." *HLQ*, 15 (1952), 283–89.

1160 CAMERON, A. B. "Donne and Dryden: Their Achievements in the Verse Epistle." *Discourse*, 11 (1968), 252–56.

1161 JORDAN, J. "The Early Verse-Letters of John Donne." *UR*, 2 (1962), 3–24.

1162 LEIN, C. D. "Donne's 'The Storme': The Poem and the Tradition." *ELR*, 4 (1974), 137–63.

1163 McGOWAN, M. M. " 'As Through a Looking-Glass': Donne's Epithalamia and Their Courtly Contest." See **996.**

1164 NELLIST, B. F. "Donne's 'Storm' and 'Calm' and the Descriptive Tradition." *MLR*, 59 (1964), 511–15.

1165 NOVARR, D. "Donne's 'Epithalamion Made at Lincoln's Inn': Context and Date." *RES*, 7 (1956), 250–63.

1166 STAPLETON, L. "The Theme of Virtue in Donne's Verse Epistles." *SP*, 55 (1958), 187–200.

1167 THOMPSON, P. "Donne and the Poetry of Patronage: The Verse Letters." See **996.**

Anniversaries

1168 ALLEN, D. C. "Donne among the Giants [in the *First Anniversary*]." *MLN*, 61 (1946), 257–60.

1169 ALLEN, D. C. "John Donne and the Tower of Babel [in the *Second Anniversary*]." *MLN*, 64 (1949), 481–83.

1170 ANSELMENT, R. A. " 'Ascensio Mendax, Descensio Crudelis': The Image of Babel in the *Anniversaries.*" *ELH*, 38 (1971), 188–205.

1171 BELLETTE, A. F. "Art and Imitation in Donne's *Anniversaries.*" *SEL*, 15 (1975), 83–96.

1172 COLIE, R. L. "The Rhetoric of Transcendence. I. Traditions of Paradox in Renaissance Verse-Epistemologies. II. John Donne's Anniversary Poems and Paradoxes of Epistemology." *PQ*, 43 (1964), 145–70.

1173 COLIE, R. L. " 'All in Peeces': Problems of Interpretation in Donne's Anniversary Poems." See **943.**

1174 ELLIOTT, E. B., Jr. "Persona and Parody in Donne's *The Anniversaries.*" *QJS*, 58 (1972), 48–57.

1175 FOX, R. A. "Donne's *Anniversaries* and the Art of Living." *ELH*, 38 (1971), 528–41.

1176 HARDISON, O. B., Jr. "The Idea of Elizabeth Drury." See **95.**

1177 HUGHES, R. E. "The Woman in Donne's *Anniversaries.*" *ELH,* 34 (1967), 307–26.

1178 HYNES, S. L. "A Note on Donne [in the *First Anniversary*] and Aquinas." *MLR,* 48 (1953), 179–81.

1179 KREPS, B. "The Serpent and Christian Paradox in Donne's 'First Anniversary.' " *RLMC,* 24 (1971), 199–207.

1180 LEBANS, W. M. "Donne's *Anniversaries* and the Tradition of Funeral Elegy." *ELH,* 39 (1972), 545–59.

1181 LEWALSKI, B. K. *Donne's "Anniversaries" and the Poetry of Praise: The Creation of a Symbolic Mode.* Princeton: Princeton University Press, 1973.

1182 LOVE, H. "The Argument of Donne's *First Anniversary.*" *MP,* 64 (1966), 125–31.

1183 MAHONY, P. "The Anniversaries: Donne's Rhetorical Approach To Evil." *JEGP,* 68 (1969), 407–13.

1184 MAHONY, P. "The Heroic Couplet in Donne's *Anniversaries.*" *Style,* 4 (1970), 107–17.

1185 MAHONY, P. "The Structure of Donne's *Anniversaries* as Companion Poems." *Genre,* 5 (1972), 235–56.

1186 MANLEY, F. "John Donne: *The Anniversaries.*" See **878** and **887.**

1187 MARSHALL, W. H. "Elizabeth Drury and the Heathens." *N&Q,* 5 (1958), 533–34.

1188 MARSHALL, W. H. "A Possible Interpretation of Donne's 'The Second Anniversary' (Lines 33–36)." *N&Q,* 5 (1958), 540–41.

1189 MARTZ, L. L. "John Donne in Meditation: *The Anniversaries.*" *ELH,* 14 (1947), 247–73; New York: Haskell House, 1970; and see **196, 206, 944,** and **958.**

1190 MAUD, R. "Donne's *First Anniversary.*" *BUSE,* 11 (1956), 218–25.

1191 QUINN, D. "Donne's *Anniversaries* as Celebration." *SEL,* 9 (1969), 97–105.

1192 SICHERMAN, C. M. "Donne's Timeless *Anniversaries.*" *UTQ,* 39 (1969–70), 127–43.

1193 STANWOOD, P. G. " 'Essential Joye' in Donne's *Anniversaries.*" *TSLL,* 13 (1971), 227–38.

1194 VOSS, A. E. "The Structure of Donne's *Anniversaries.*" *ESA,* 12 (1969), 1–30.

1195 WILLIAMSON, G. "The Design of Donne's *Anniversaries.*" *MP,* 60 (1963), 183–91; and see **139.**

Divine Poems and Epicedes

1196 ALLEN, D. C. "John Donne's 'Paradise and Calvarie.' " *MLN,* 60 (1945), 398–400.

1197 ANDERSON, D. K., Jr. "Donne's 'Hymne to God my God, in my Sicknesse' and the T-in-O Maps." *SAQ,* 71 (1972), 459–594.

1198 ARCHER, S. "Meditation and the Structure of Donne's 'Holy Sonnets.' " *ELH*, 28 (1961), 137−47; and see **878.**

1199 BAKER-SMITH, D. "John Donne and the *Mysterium Crucis*." *EM*, 19 (1968), 65−82.

1200 BECK, R. "A Precedent for Donne's Imagery in Good Friday, 1613. Riding Westward.' " *RES*, 19 (1968), 166−69.

1201 BELL, A. H. "Donne's Atonement Conceit in the *Holy Sonnets*." *Cresset*, 32, vii (1969), 15−17.

1202 CAMPBELL, H. M. "Donne's 'Hymn to God, My God, in My Sickness.' " *CE*, 5 (1944), 192−96.

1203 CHAMBERS, A. B. "The Meaning of the 'Temple' in Donne's *La Corona*." *JEGP*, 59 (1960), 212−17.

1204 CHAMBERS, A. B. " 'Goodfriday, 1613. Riding Westward': The Poem and the Tradition." *ELH*, 28 (1961), 31−53.

1205 CLEMENTS, A. L. "Donne's Holy Sonnet XIV." *MLN*, 76 (1961), 484−89; and see **878.**

1206 CORNELIUS, D. K. "Donne's 'Holy Sonnet XIV.' " *Expl*, 24 (1965), Item 25.

1207 ESCH, A. "Paradise and Calvary." *Anglia*, 78 (1960), 74−77.

1208 FAUSSET, H. L. "Donne's Holy Sonnets." *Poets and Pundits*. London: Cape, 1947.

1209 FRANCIS, W. N. "Donne's 'Goodfriday 1613. Riding Westward.' " *Expl*, 13 (1955), Item 21.

1210 FRENCH, A. L. "The Psychopathology of Donne's *Holy Sonnets*." *CR*, 13 (1970), 111−24.

1211 FRIEDMAN, D. M. "Memory and the Art of Salvation in Donne's Good Friday Poem." *ELR*, 3 (1973), 418−42.

1212 GARDNER, H. "The Religious Poetry of John Donne." See **878, 888,** and **944.**

1213 GOLDBERG, J. S. "Donne's Journey East: Aspects of a Seventeenth-Century Trope." *SP*, 68 (1971), 470−83.

1214 GRANT, P. "Augustinian Spirituality and the *Holy Sonnets* of John Donne." *ELH*, 38 (1971), 542−61; and see **178.**

1215 GRENANDER, M. E. "Holy Sonnets VIII and XVII: John Donne." *BUSE*, 4 (1960), 95−105.

1216 GRENANDER, M. E. "Donne's *Holy Sonnets, XII*." *Expl*, 13 (1955), Item 42.

1217 HAZO, S. "Donne's Divine Letter: ['The Crosse']. *Essays and Studies in Language and Literature*, ed. H. H. Petit. Pittsburgh: Duquesne University Press, 1964.

1218 HEIST, W. W. "Donne on Divine Grace: Holy Sonnet No. XIV." *PMASAL*, 53 (1968), 311−20.

1219 HERMAN, G. "Donne's *Holy Sonnets, XIV*." *Expl*, 12 (1954), Item 18; and see **878.**

1220 HERMAN, G. "Donne's 'Good-Friday, 1613. Riding Westward.' " *Expl*, 14 (1956), Item 60.

1221 KIRKPATRICK, H. "Donne's 'Upon the Annunciation and Passion Falling upon One Day, 1608.' " *Expl*, 30 (1972), Item 39.

1222 KNOX, G. "Donne's *Holy Sonnets*, XIV." *Expl*, 15 (1956), Item 2; and see **878.**

1223 LEVENSON, J. C. "Donne's *Holy Sonnets*, XIV." *Expl*, 11 (1953), Item 31; and see **878.**

1224 LEVENSON, J. C. "Donne's *Holy Sonnets*, XIV." *Expl*, 12 (1954), Item 36; and see **878.**

1225 MARTZ, L. L. "Donne's 'Holy Sonnets' and 'Good Friday, 1613.' " See **206** and **878.**

1226 MUELLER, W. R. "Donne's Adulterous Female Town." *MLN*, 76 (1961), 312−14.

1227 NEWTON, W. "A Study of Donne's *Sonnet XIV*." *ATR*, 41 (1959), 10−12.

1228 PARISH, J. E. "Donne's *Holy Sonnets*, XIII." *Expl*, 22 (1963), Item 19.

1229 PARISH, J. E. "No. 14 of Donne's *Holy Sonnets*." *CE*, 24 (1963), 299−302; and see **878.**

1230 PETERSON, D. L. "John Donne's 'Holy Sonnets' and the Anglican Doctrine of Contrition." *SP*, 56 (1959), 504−18.

1231 RUOTOLO, L. P. "The Trinitarian Framework of Donne's Holy Sonnet XIV." *JHI*, 27 (1966), 445−46.

1232 SHERWOOD, T. G. "Reason, Faith, and Just Augustinian Lamentation in Donne's Elegy on Prince Henry." *SEL*, 13 (1973), 53−67.

1233 STEIG, M. "Donne's Divine Rapist: Unconscious Fantasy in Holy Sonnet XIV." *HSL*, 4 (1972), 52−58.

1234 TOURNEY, L. D. "Convention and Wit in Donne's *Elegie* on Prince Henry." *SP*, 71 (1974), 473−83.

1235 WALLERSTEIN, R. C. "Rhetoric in the English Renaissance: Two Elegies [Donne's on Prince Henry and Milton's *Lycidas*]." *English Institute Essays of 1948*, ed. D. A. Robertson, Jr. New York: Columbia University Press, 1949.

1236 WALLERSTEIN, R. "The Death of Prince Henry." See **254.**

Studies: Prose

1237 ALLEN, D. C. "Dean Donne Sets His Text." *ELH*, 10 (1943), 208−29.

1238 ANDREASEN, N. J. C. "Donne's *Devotions* and the Psychology of Assent." *MP*, 62 (1965), 207−16.

1239 ANGLO, S. "More Machiavellian than Machiavel: A Study of the Context of Donne's *Conclave*." See **996.**

1240 BOSTON, R. "The Variable Heart in Donne's Sermons." *CSR*, 2 (1971), 36−41.

1241 CARRITHERS, G. H., Jr. *Donne at Sermons: A Christian Existential World.* Albany: State University of New York Press, 1972.

1242 COX, G. H., III. "Donne's *Devotions:* A Meditative Sequence on Repentance." *HTR*, 66 (1973), 331—51.

1243 DANIEL, E. R. "Reconciliation, Covenant and Election: A Study in the Theology of John Donne." *ATR*, 48 (1966), 14—30.

1244 DOEBLER, B. A. "Donne's Debt to the Great Traditions: Old and New in His Testament of Death." *Anglia,* 85 (1967), 15—33.

1245 DOEBLER, B. A. *The Quickening Seed: Death in the Sermons of John Donne.* Salzburg: Universitat Salzburg, 1974.

1246 ELIOT, T. S. "Lancelot Andrewes." See **86.**

1247 GERALDINE, Sr. M. "Erasmus and the Tradition of Paradox." *SP*, 61 (1964), 41—63.

1248 GIFFORD, W. "John Donne's Sermons on the 'Grand Days.' " *HLQ,* 29 (1966), 235—44.

1249 GIFFORD, W. "Time and Place in Donne's Sermons." *PMLA,* 82 (1967), 388—98.

1250 GOLDBERG, J. A. "The Understanding of Sickness in Donne's *Devotions.*" *RenQ,* 24 (1971), 507—17.

1251 HARDING, D. W. "The *Devotions* Now." See **996.**

1252 HASSEL, R. C., Jr. "Donne's *Ignatius His Conclave* and the New Astronomy." *MP,* 68 (1971), 329—37.

1253 HAYWARD, J. "A Note on Donne the Preacher." See **997.**

1254 HEATHERINGTON, M. E. " 'Decency' and 'Zeal' in the Sermons of John Donne." *TSLL,* 9 (1967), 307—16.

1255 HICKEY, R. L. "Donne's Art of Preaching." *UTSH,* 1 (1956), 65—74.

1256 KRUEGER, R. "The Publication of John Donne's Sermons." *RES,* 15 (1964), 151—60.

1257 LANDER, C. "A Dangerous Sickness Which Turned to a Spotted Fever: [*Devotions*]." *SEL,* 11 (1971), 89—108.

1258 LOWE, I. "John Donne and The Middle Way: The Reason-Faith Equation in Donne's Sermons." *JHI,* 22 (1961), 389—97.

1259 MAHOOD, M. M. "Donne: The Baroque Preacher." See **204.**

1260 MALLOCH, A. E. "Donne's *Pseudo-Martyr* and *Catalogus Librorum Aulicorum.*" *MLN,* 70 (1955), 174—75.

1261 MALLOCH, A. E. "The Techniques and Function of the Renaissance Paradox." *SP,* 53 (1956), 191—203.

1262 MALLOCH, A. E. "The Definition of Sin in Donne's *Biathanatos.*" *MLN,* 72 (1957), 332—35.

1263 MANN, L. A. "The Marriage Analogue of Letter and Spirit in Donne's Devotional Prose." *JEGP,* 70 (1971), 607—16.

1264 MERCHANT, W. M. "Donne's Sermon to the Virginia Company." See **996.**

1265 MERRILL, T. F. "John Donne and the Word of God." *NM,* 69 (1968), 597—616.

1266 MITCHELL, W. F. "Andrewes, the 'Witty' Preachers, and Donne." See **469.**

JOHN DONNE

1267 MUELLER, J. M. "The Exegesis of Experience: Dean Donne's *Devotions upon Emergent Occasions*." *JEGP*, 67 (1968), 1—19.

1268 MUELLER, W. R. *John Donne, Preacher*. Princeton: Princeton University Press, 1962.

1269 MURPHY, J. "The Young Donne and the Senecan Amble." *BRMMLA*, 23 (1969), 163—67.

1270 NICOLSON, M. H. "Kepler, the *Somnium*, and John Donne." *JHI*, 1 (1940), 259—80; and see **116.**

1271 PHELPS, G. "The Prose of Donne. . . . " See **7.**

1272 QUINN, D. B. "Donne's Christian Eloquence." *ELH*, 27 (1960), 276—97; and see **276.**

1273 QUINN, D. B. "John Donne's Principles of Biblical Exegesis." *JEGP*, 61 (1962), 313—29.

1274 RASPA, A. "Theology and Poetry in Donne's *Conclave*." *ELH*, 32 (1965), 478—89.

1275 ROONEY, W. J. J. "John Donne's 'Second Prebend Sermon': A Stylistic Analysis." *TSLL*, 4 (1962), 24—34; and see **276.**

1276 SCHLEINER, W. *The Imagery of John Donne's Sermons*. Providence: Brown University Press, 1970.

1277 SHAPIRO, I. A. "Walton and the Occasion of Donne's *Devotions*." *RES*, 9 (1958), 18—22.

1278 SHERWOOD, T. G. "Reason in Donne's Sermons." *ELH*, 39 (1972), 353—74.

1279 SIEGEL, P. N. "Donne's *Paradoxes and Problems*." *PQ*, 28 (1949), 507—11.

1280 SIMPSON, E. M. *A Study of the Prose Works of John Donne*. Oxford: Clarendon Press, 1924; second edition, 1948.

1281 SIMPSON, E. M. "The Biographical Value of Donne's Sermons." *RES*, 2 (1951), 339—57.

1282 SIMPSON, E. M. "The Literary Value of Donne's Sermons." See **905** and **944.**

1283 SIMPSON, E. M. "Donne's 'Paradoxes and Problems.' " See **997.**

1284 SOWTON, I. "Religious Opinion in the Prose Letters of John Donne." *Canadian Journal of Theology*, 6 (1960), 179—90.

1285 SPARROW, J. "Donne and Contemporary Preachers." *E&S*, 16 (1931), 144—78.

1286 STAPLETON, L. "John Donne: The Moment of the Sermon." See **284.**

1287 UMBACH, H. H. "The Rhetoric of Donne's Sermons." *PMLA*, 52 (1937), 354—58.

1288 UMBACH, H. H. "The Merit of Metaphysical Style in Donne's Easter Sermons." *ELH*, 12 (1945), 108—29.

1289 VAN LAAN, T. F. "John Donne's *Devotions* and the Jesuit Spiritual Exercises." *SP*, 60 (1963), 191—202.

1290 WEBBER, J. The Prose Styles of John Donne's *Devotions upon Emergent Occasions*." *Anglia*, 79 (1961—62), 138—52.

1291 WEBBER, J. *Contrary Music: The Prose Style of John Donne.* Madison: University of Wisconsin Press, 1963.

1292 WEBBER, J. "Donne and Bunyan: The Styles of Two Faiths." See **276** and **287**.

William Drummond (1585— 1649)

Editions

1293 *Poems: 1616.* Amsterdam: Theatrum Orbis Terrarum, 1969.

1294 *The Poems,* ed. T. Maitland. Edinburgh: Ballantyne, 1832; New York: AMS Press, 1971.

1295 *The Poetical Works,* ed. L. E. Kastner. Manchester: Manchester University Press, 1913.

1296 *The Works:[1711],* ed. J. Sage and T. Ruddiman. New York: Olm, 1970.

1297 *Conversations.* See **1662** and **1672—74.**

1298 *A Cyprus Grove,* ed. S. Clegg. London: Hawthornden, 1919.

1299. *Forth Feasting: 1617.* Amsterdam: Theatrum Orbis Terrarum, 1969.

1300 *A Midnight's Trance,* ed. R. Ellrodt. Oxford: Blackwell, 1951.

Studies

1301 ELLRODT, R. "More Drummond Borrowings." *HLQ,* 16 (1952—53), 305—10.

1302 FOGLE, F. R. *A Critical Study of William Drummond of Hawthornden.* New York: Columbia University Press, 1952.

1303 FRITZ, H. "Drummond's Authentic Voice." *LHR,* 9 (1967), 16—38.

1304 JACK, R. D. S. "Drummond of Hawthornden: The Major Scottish Sources." *SSL,* 6 (1969), 36—46.

1305 JOLY, A. *William Drummond de Hawthornden.* Lille: Douriez-Battaille, 1934.

1306 MacDONALD, R. H. "Drummond of Hawthornden, Miss Euphemia Kyninghame, and the 'Poems.' " *MLR,* 60 (1965), 494—99.

1307 MacDONALD, R. H. "Drummond of Hawthornden: The Season at Bourges, 1607." *CompD,* 4 (1970), 89—109.

1308 MacDONALD, R. H. "A Disputed Maxim of State in 'Forth Feasting.' " *JHI,* 32 (1971), 295—98.

1309 MacDONALD, R. H. *The Library of Drummond of Hawthornden.* Edinburgh: Edinburgh University Press, 1971.

1310 MACLEAN, C. M. *Alexander Scott, Montgomerie, and Drummond of Hawthornden as Lyric Poets*. Cambridge: Cambridge University Press, 1915.

1311 MASSON, D. *Drummond of Hawthornden*. London: Macmillan, 1873; New York: Haskell House, 1969.

1312 McDIARMID, M. P. "The Spanish Plunder of William Drummond of Hawthornden." *MLR*, 44 (1949), 17−25.

1313 RUGOFF, M. A. "Drummond's Debt to Donne." *PQ*, 16 (1937), 85−88.

1314 SMITH, G. "The Influence of Sir John Hayward and Joshua Sylvester upon William Drummond's 'Cypresse Grove.' " *PQ*, 26 (1947), 69−80.

1315 STAINER, C. L. *Jonson and Drummond, Their Conversations*. Oxford: Blackwell, 1925.

1316 WALLERSTEIN, R. C. "The Style of Drummond of Hawthornden in Its Relation to his Translations." *PMLA*, 48 (1933), 1090−1107.

John Earle (1600?− 1665)

Editions

1317 *Micro-cosmographie*, ed. E. Arber. London: Rider, 1869; New York: AMS Press, 1966.

1318 *Micro-Cosmographie*, ed. G. Murphy. London: Golden Cockerel, 1928.

1319 *Microcosmography*, ed. H. Osborne. London: University Tutorial Press, 1933.

1320 *Microcosmography*, ed. A. S. West. Cambridge: Cambridge University Press, 1897, 1951.

1321 *A Book of 'Characters,'* ed. R. Aldington. London: Routledge; New York: Dutton, 1924.

1322 *A Cabinet of Characters*, ed. G. Murphy. London: Milford, 1925; St. Clair Shores: Scholarly Press, 1972.

1323 *A Mirror of Charactery*, ed. H. Osborne, London: University Tutorial Press, 1933.

Studies

1324 BOYCE, B. "The Theory and the Vogue of the Character: From Causaubon to Earle." See **270**.

1325 BOYCE, B. *The Polemic Character, 1640− 1661*. Lincoln: University of Nebraska Press, 1955.

1326 CLAUSEN, W. "The Beginnings of English Character-Writing in the Early Seventeenth Century." *PQ*, 25 (1946), 32−45.

1327 SMITH, D. N. *Characters of the Seventeenth Century.* Oxford: Clarendon Press, 1918.

1328 THOMPSON, E. N. S. "Character Books." *Literary Bypaths of the Renaissance.* New Haven: Yale University Press, 1924; Freeport: Books for Libraries, 1968.

Owen Felltham (1602?– 1668)

Editions

1329 *The Poems of Owen Felltham,* ed. T.-L. Pebworth and C. J. Summers. University Park: *Seventeenth-Century News, Editions and Studies,* 1974.

1330 *Resolves: Divine, Morall and Political,* ed. O. Smeaton. London: Dent, 1904.

Studies

1331 BOYCE, B. *The Polemic Character, 1640– 1661.* Lincoln: University of Nebraska Press, 1955.

1332 HAZLETT, M. "New Frame and Various Composition: Development of the Form of Owen Felltham's *Resolves.*" *MP,* 51 (1953), 93– 101.

1333 ROBERTSON, J. "The Use Made of Owen Felltham's 'Resolves': A Study in Plagiarism." MLR, 39 (1944), 108– 15.

1334 ROBERTSON, J. "Felltham's *Character of the Low Countries.*" *MLN,* 58 (1943), 385– 88.

1335 STAPLETON, L. "The Graces and the Muses: Felltham's *Resolves.*" See **284.**

1336 TUPPER, F. S. "New Facts Regarding Owen Felltham." *MLN,* 54 (1939), 199– 201.

Giles and Phineas Fletcher
(1588– 1623; 1582– 1650)

Editions

1337 *The Poetical Works of Giles and Phineas Fletcher,* ed. F. S. Boas. Cambridge: Cambridge University Press, 1908– 9, 1970.

1338 *Venus and Anchises,* ed. E. Seaton. Oxford: Oxford University Press, 1926.

Studies

1339 BALDWIN, R. G. "Phineas Fletcher: His Modern Readers and his Renaissance Ideas." *PQ*, 40 (1961), 462—75.

1340 CORY, H. E. *Spenser, the School of the Fletchers, and Milton.* Berkeley: University of California Press, 1912.

1341 ESCH, A. "Structure and Style in Some Minor Religious Epics. . . . " See **173.**

1342 GRUNDY, J. "Giles and Phineas Fletcher." See **179.**

1343 HOLADAY, A. G. "Giles Fletcher and the Puritans." *JEGP*, 54 (1955), 578—86.

1344 HOLADAY, A. G. "Giles Fletcher and the Catholics." See **68.**

1345 KURTH, B. O. "New Testament Narratives." *Milton and Christian Heroism.* Berkeley: University of California Press, 1959.

1346 LANGDALE, A. B. *Phineas Fletcher: Man of Letters, Science and Divinity.* New York: Columbia University Press, 1937.

1347 TILLYARD, E. M. W. "The Spenserians." *The English Epic and Its Background.* London: Chatto & Windus, 1954.

Thomas Fuller (1608— 1661)

Editions

1348 *The History of the Worthies of England,* ed. A. Nuttall, London: Tegg, 1840.

1349 *The Worthies of England,* ed. J. Freeman. London: Allen & Unwin, 1952; New York: Barnes & Noble, 1962.

1350 *The Holy and Profane State,* ed. M. C. Walten. New York: Columbia University Press, 1938.

1351 *Selections,* ed. E. K. Broadus. Oxford: Clarendon Press, 1928.

1352 *Thoughts and Contemplations,* ed. J. O. Wood. London: S.P.C.K., 1964.

1353 *A Book of Characters,* ed. R. Aldington, London: Routledge; New York: Dutton, 1924.

Studies

1354 ADDISON, J. T. "Thomas Fuller, Historian and Humorist." *Historical Magazine of the Protestant Episcopal Church,* 21 (1952), 100—147.

1355 ADDISON, W. *Worthy Dr. Fuller.* London: Dent, 1951.

1356 HOUGHTON, W. E. *The Formation of Thomas Fuller's "Holy and Profane States."* Cambridge: Harvard University Press, 1938.

1357 LYMAN, D. B. *The Great Tom Fuller.* Berkeley: University of California Press, 1935.

1358 MITCHELL, W. F. "Thomas Fuller." See **469.**

1359 RESNICK, R. B. "Thomas Fuller: Doctor of the Sugar-Coated Pill." *LHR,* 6 (1964), 53 – 68.

1360 RESNICK, R. B. "Thomas Fuller's Pulpit Wit." *XUS,* 4 (1965), 109 – 23.

1361 RESNICK, R. B. "An Ounce of Mirth: The Function of Thomas Fuller's Wit." *CLAJ,* 11 (1967), 123 – 34.

1362 RESNICK, R. B. "The Wit of Biblical Allusion and Imagery in Thomas Fuller." *Greyfriar,* 10 (1968), 16 – 24.

1363 ROBERTS, S. C. *Thomas Fuller, A Seventeenth-Century Worthy.* Manchester: Manchester University Press, 1953.

1364 THOMPSON, E. N. S. "Character Books." *Literary Bypaths of the Renaissance.* New Haven: Yale University Press, 1924; Freeport: Books for Libraries, 1968.

Joseph Hall (1574 – 1656)

Editions

1365 *Works,* ed. P. Wynter, 10 vols. Oxford: Oxford University Press, 1863; New York: AMS Press, 1969.

1366 *Collected Poems,* ed. A. Davenport. Liverpool: Liverpool University Press, 1969.

1367 *Heaven upon Earth and Characters of Vertues and Vices,* ed. R. Kirk. New Brunswick: Rutgers University Press, 1948.

1368 *A Book of Characters,* ed. R. Aldington. London: Routledge; New York: Dutton, 1924.

1369 *A Cabinet of Characters,* ed. G. Murphy. London: Milford, 1925; St. Clair Shores: Scholarly Press, 1972.

1370 *A Mirror of Charactery,* ed. H. Osborne. London: University Tutorial Press, 1933.

Studies

1371 BOYCE, B. "Joseph Hall's *Characters of Vertues and Vices.*" See **270.**

1372 BOYCE, B. *The Polemic Character, 1640 – 1661.* Lincoln: University of Nebraska Press, 1955.

1373 CHEW, A. "Joseph Hall and Neo-Stoicism." *PMLA*, 65 (1950), 1130—45.

1374 CLAUSEN, W. See **1326.**

1375 HALL, J. H., III. "Joseph Hall, the English Seneca and Champion of Episcopacy." *Historical Magazine of the Protestant Episcopal Church*, 21 (1952), 62—99.

1376 HARRIS, B. "Men Like Satyrs." *Elizabethan Poetry: Stratford-upon Avon Studies*, 2 (1960), 175—201.

1377 JENSEN, E. J. "Hall and Marston: The Role of the Satirist." *SNL*, 4 (1967), 72—83.

1378 KIRK, R. "A Seventeenth-Century Controversy: Extremism vs. Moderation." *TSLL*, 9 (1967), 1—35.

1379 MULLER-SCHWEFE, G. "Joseph Hall's *Characters of Vertues and Vices:* Notes Towards a Revaluation." *TSLL*, 14 (1972), 235—51.

1380 SMITH, P. A. "Bishop Hall, 'Our English Seneca.' " *PMLA*, 63 (1948), 1191—1204.

1381 STEIN, A. "Joseph Hall's Imitation of Juvenal." *MLR*, 43 (1948), 315—22.

1382 THOMPSON, E. N. S. "Character Books." *Literary Bypaths of the Renaissance.* New Haven: Yale University Press, 1924; Freeport: Books for Libraries, 1968.

Edward, Lord Herbert of Cherbury (1583— 1648)

Editions

1383 *The Autobiography,* ed. C. H. Herford. Newtown: Gregynog Press, 1928.

1384 *The Autobiography,* ed. S. Lee. London: Gibbings, 1892, 1906; Westport: Greenwood, 1970.

1385 *De Religione Laici,* ed. H. R. Hutcheson. New Haven: Yale University Press, 1944.

1386 *De Veritate,* ed. M. H. Carré. Bristol: Arrowsmith, 1937.

1387 *The Poems,* ed. J. C. Collins. London: Chatto & Windus, 1881; Folcroft: Folcroft Library Editions, 1971.

1388 *Poems,* ed. G. C. M. Smith. New York: Oxford University Press, 1923.

Bibliographies

1389 BERRY, L. E., ed. "Edward, Lord Herbert of Cherbury: [Bibliography]." See **4.**

1390 SPENCER, T., ed. "Edward, Lord Herbert of Cherbury: [Bibliography]." See **17.**

Studies

1391 BOTTRALL, M. "Lord Herbert of Cherbury." See **269.**

1392 DART, T. "Lord Herbert of Cherbury's Lute Book." *Music and Letters,* 38 (1957), 136—48.

1393 EBNER, D. "Herbert of Cherbury." See **275.**

1393a GRIERSON, H. J. C. "Edward, Lord Herbert." *MLR*, 21 (1926), 210—13.

1394 HANFORD, J. H. "Lord Herbert of Cherbury and His Son." *HLQ*, 5 (1942), 317—32.

1395 HEBERT, C. A. "The Platonic Love Poetry of Lord Herbert of Cherbury." *BSUF,* 11, ii (1971), 46—50.

1396 HOEY, J. "A Study of Lord Herbert of Cherbury's Poetry." *RMS*, 14 (1970), 69—89.

1397 KEISTER, D. A. "Donne and Herbert of Cherbury: An Exchange of Verses." *MLQ*, 8 (1947), 430—34.

1398 LYTTLE, C. "Lord Herbert of Cherbury, Apostle of Ethical Deism." *CH*, 4 (1935), 247—67.

1399 MERCHANT, W. M. "Lord Herbert of Cherbury and Seventeenth-Century Historical Writing." *Transactions of the Honourable Society of Cymmrodorion,* Session 1956 (1957), 47—63.

1400 RICKEY, M. E. "Rhymecraft in Edward and George Herbert." *JEGP*, 57 (1958), 502—11.

1401 WILLEY, B. "Lord Herbert of Cherbury: A Spiritual Quixote of the Seventeenth Century." *E&S*, 27 (1941), 22—29.

1402 WILLEY, B. "Rational Theology: Lord Herbert of Cherbury." See **136.**

George Herbert (1593— 1633)

Editions

1403 *The Works,* ed. F. E. Hutchinson. Oxford: Clarendon Press, 1941.

1404 *The English Works,* ed. G. H. Palmer. Boston: Houghton-Mifflin, 1908.

1405 *The English Poems,* ed. C. A. Patrides. London: Dent, 1974; Totowa: Roman & Littlefield, 1975.

1406 *The Poems,* ed. H. Gardner. London: Oxford University Press, 1961.

1407 [Selected Poems], ed. D. Fitts. New York: Dell, 1962.

1408 *Selected Poetry,* ed. J. H. Summers. New York: New American Library, 1971.

1409 *Selected Poems,* ed. G. Reeves. New York: Barnes & Noble, 1971.

1410 *The Temple*, ed. F. Meynell. London: Nonesuch; New York: Random House, 1927.

1411 *The Temple and A Priest to the Temple*, ed. E. Thomas. London: Dent, 1927.

1412 *The Country Parson and Selected Poems*. London: S.C.M. Press, 1956.

1413 *The Country Parson*, ed. H. C. Beeching. New York: Longmans; Oxford: Blackwell, 1898, 1915.

1414 *The Priest to the Temple; or, The Country Parson*. Milwaukee: Morehouse, 1916.

1415 *The Country Parson*, ed. G. M. Forbes. London: Faith, 1949.

1416 *The Latin Poetry, A Bilingual Edition*, ed. M. McCloskey and P. R. Murphy, Athens: Ohio University Press, 1965.

Bibliographies and Concordance

1417 BERRY, L. E., ed. "George Herbert: [Bibliography]." See **4.**

1418 BOTTRALL, M., ed. "Herbert, 1593–1633: [Bibliography]." See **6.**

1419 MANN, C., ed. *A Concordance to the English Poems of George Herbert.* New York: Houghton-Mifflin, 1927.

1420 SPENCER, T., ed. "George Herbert: [Bibliography]." See **17.**

1421 TANNENBAUM, S. A. and D. R., eds. *George Herbert: A Concise Bibliography. Elizabethan Bibliographies*, No. 35. Port Washington: Kennikat, 1967.

Studies

1422 ALLEN, D. S. "George Herbert: 'The Rose.' " See **142.**

1423 ASALS, H. "The Voice of George Herbert's 'The Church.' " *ELH*, 36 (1969), 511–28.

1424 ASALS, H. "The Tetragrammaton in *The Temple.*" *SCN*, 31 (1973), 48–50.

1425 BEACHCROFT, T. O. "Nicholas Ferrar: His Influence on and Friendship with George Herbert." *Criterion*, 12 (1932), 24–42.

1426 BENJAMIN, E. B. "Herbert's *Vertue.*" *Expl*, 9 (1950), Item 12.

1427 BENNETT, J. "George Herbert." See **148.**

1428 BLANCHARD, M. M. "The Leap into Darkness: Donne, Herbert, and God." *Ren*, 17 (1964), 38–50.

1429 BLAU, S. D. "The Poet as Casuist: Herbert's 'Church-Porch.' " *Genre*, 4 (1971), 142–52.

1430 BOTTRALL, M. *George Herbert.* London: Murray, 1954; and see **196.**

1431 BOWERS, F. "Herbert's Sequential Imagery: 'The Temper.' " *MP*, 59 (1962), 202 – 13.

1432 BRADBROOK, M.C. "The Liturgical Tradition in English Verse: Herbert and Eliot." *Theology*, 44 (1942), 13 – 23.

1433 BROWN, C. C., and W. P. INGOLDSBY. "George Herbert's 'Easter-Wings.' " *HLQ*, 35 (1972), 131 – 42.

1434 CARNES, V. "The Unity of George Herbert's *The Temple:* A Reconsideration." *ELH*, 35 (1968), 505 – 26.

1435 CARPENTER, M. "From Herbert to Marvell: Poetics in 'A Wreath' and 'The Coronet.' " *JEGP*, 69 (1970), 155 – 69.

1436 CHAMPION, L. S. "Body Versus Soul in George Herbert's 'The Collar.' " *Style*, 1 (1967), 131 – 37.

1437 CHUTE, M. *Two Gentlemen: The Lives of George Herbert and Robert Herrick.* New York: Dutton, 1959.

1438 CLARK, I. " 'Lord, in Thee the *Beauty* Lies in the Discovery': 'Love Unknown' and Reading Herbert." *ELH*, 39 (1972), 560 – 84.

1439 CLEMENTS, A. L. "Theme, Tone, and Tradition in George Herbert's Poetry." *ELR*, 3 (1973), 264 – 83.

1440 COLIE, R. L. "*Logos in The Temple:* George Herbert and the Shape of Content." *JWCI*, 26 (1963), 327 – 42; and see **79**.

1441 EL-GABALWY, S. "The Pilgrimage: George Herbert's Favourite Allegorical Technique." *CLAJ*, 13 (1970), 408 – 19.

1442 EL-GABALWY, S. "George Herbert's Affinities with the Homiletical Mode." *HAB*, 21, iii (1970), 38 – 48.

1443 EL-GABALWY, S. "George Herbert and the *Ars Amatoria.*" *XUS*, 10 (1971), 93 – 102.

1444 EL-GABALWY, S. "A Seventeenth-Century Reading of George Herbert." *PLL*, 7 (1971), 159 – 67.

1445 ELIOT, T. S. *George Herbert.* London, New York: Longmans, Green, 1962.

1446 ENDICOTT, A. M. "The Structure of George Herbert's *Temple:* A Reconsideration." *UTQ*, 34 (1964 – 65), 226 – 37.

1447 ERDE, F. VON "George Herbert's 'The Sonne': In Defense of the English Language." *SEL*, 12 (1972), 173 – 82.

1448 ERICKSON, E. E., Jr. "A Structural Approach to Imagery." *Style*, 3 (1969), 227 – 47.

1449 EVANS, G. B. "George Herbert's 'Jordan.' " *N&Q*, 5 (1958), 215.

1450 FISH, S. E. "Letting Go: The Reader in Herbert's Poetry." *ELH*, 37 (1970), 475 – 94, and see **88**.

1451 FISH, S. E. "Catechizing the Reader: Herbert's Socratean Rhetoric." See **241**.

1452 FREEMAN, R. "George Herbert and the Emblem Books." *RES*, 17 (1941), 150 – 65; and see **89**.

1453 FREEMAN, R. "Parody as a Literary Form: George Herbert and Wilfred Owen." *EIC*, 13 (1963), 307 – 22.

1454 FREER, C. *Music for a King: George Herbert's Style and the Metrical Psalms.* Baltimore: Johns Hopkins Press, 1972.

1455 GALLAGHER, M. P. "Rhetoric, Style, and George Herbert." *ELH,* 37 (1970), 495—516.

1456 GASKELL, R. "Herbert's 'Vanitie.' " *CritQ,* 3 (1961), 313—15.

1457 GRANT, P. "Augustinian Spirituality and George Herbert's *The Temple.*" See **178.**

1458 GRANT, P. "George Herbert and Juan de Valdes: The Franciscan Mode and Protestant Manner." See **178.**

1459 GREENWOOD, E. B. "George Herbert's Sonnet 'Prayer.' " *EIC,* 15 (1965), 27—45.

1460 HANDSCOMBE, R. J. "George Herbert's 'The Collar': A Study in Frustration." *Lang&S,* 3 (1970), 29—37.

1461 HANLEY, S. W. "Temples in *The Temple*: George Herbert's Study of the Church." *SEL,* 8 (1968), 121—35.

1462 HAYES, A. M. "Counterpoint in Herbert." *SP,* 35 (1938), 43—60.

1463 HIGBIE, R. "Images of Enclosure in George Herbert's *The Temple.*" *TSLL,* 15 (1973—74), 627—38.

1464 HILL, D. M. "Allusion and Meaning in Herbert's 'Jordan I.' " *Neophil,* 56 (1972), 344—51.

1465 HOWARD, T. T. "Herbert and Crashaw: Notes on Meditative Focus." *GorR,* 11 (1968), 79—98.

1466 HUGHES, R. E. "George Herbert's Rhetorical World." *Criticism,* 3 (1961), 86—94.

1467 HUGHES, R. E. "George Herbert and the Incarnation." *Cithara,* 4, i (1964), 22—32.

1468 HUTCHINSON, F. E. "George Herbert." See **123.**

1469 JOHNSON, L. A. "The Relationship of 'The Church Militant' to *The Temple.*" *SP,* 68 (1971), 200—206.

1470 KELLIHER, W. H. [Latin Poetry.] See **150.**

1471 KNIEGER, B. "The Religious Verse of George Herbert." *CLAJ,* 4 (1960), 138—47.

1472 KNIEGER, B. "The Purchase-Sale: Patterns of Business Imagery in the Poetry of George Herbert." *SEL,* 6 (1966), 111—24.

1473 KNIGHTS, L. C. "George Herbert." See **104.**

1474 LEISHMAN, J. B. "George Herbert." See **201.**

1475 LEVANG, D. "George Herbert's 'The Church Militant' and the Chances of History." *PQ,* 36 (1957), 265—68.

1476 LEVITT, P. M., and K. G. JOHNSTON. "Herbert's 'The Collar' and the Story of Job." *PLL,* 4 (1968), 329—30.

1477 LEVITT, P. M., and K. G. JOHNSTON. "Herbert's 'The Collar': A Nautical Metaphor." *SP,* 66 (1969), 217—24.

1478 LOW, A. "Herbert's 'Jordan (I)' and the Court Masque." *Criticism,* 14 (1972), 109—18.

1479 MAHOOD, M. M. "Two Anglican Poets: [George Herbert and Christina Rossetti]." See **204.**

1480 MAHOOD, M. M. "The Nature of Herbert's Wit." *Stratford-upon-Avon Studies,* 11 (1970), 123−48.

1481 McLAUGHLIN, E., and G. THOMAS. "Communion in *The Temple.*" *SEL,* 15 (1975), 111−24.

1482 MERRILL, T. F. " 'The Sacrifice' and the Structure of Religious Language." *Lang&S,* 2 (1970), 275−87.

1483 MOLESWORTH, C. "Herbert's 'The Elixir': Revision Towards Action." *CP,* 5, ii (1972), 12−20.

1484 MOLLENKOTT, V. R. "The Many and the One in George Herbert's 'Providence.' " *CLAJ,* 10 (1966), 34−41.

1485 MOLLENKOTT, V. R. "Experimental Freedom in Herbert's Sonnets." *CSR,* 1 (1971), 109−16.

1486 MOLLENKOTT, V. R. "George Herbert's Epithet-Sonnets." *Genre,* 5 (1972), 131−37.

1487 MOLLENKOTT, V. R. "George Herbert's 'Redemption.' " *ELN,* 10 (1973), 262−67.

1488 MONTGOMERY, R. L., Jr. "The Province of Allegory in George Herbert's Verse." *TSLL,* 1 (1960), 457−72.

1489 MULDER, J. R. "George Herbert's 'The Temple': Design and Methodology." *SCN,* 31 (1973), 37−45.

1490 OSTRIKER, A. "Song and Speech in the Metrics of George Herbert." *PMLA,* 80 (1965), 62−68.

1491 PARFITT, G. A. E. "Donne, Herbert, and the Matter of Schools." *EIC,* 22 (1972), 381−95.

1492 PAYNTER, M. " 'Sinne and Love': Thematic Patterns in George Herbert's Lyrics." *YES,* 3 (1973), 85−93.

1493 PENNEL, C. A., and W. P. WILLIAMS. "The Unity of *The Temple.*" *XUS,* 5 (1966), 37−45.

1494 POLLOCK, J. J. "George Herbert's Enclosure Imagery." *SCN,* 31 (1973), 55.

1495 PRIMEAU, R. "Reading George Herbert: Process vs. Rescue." *College Literature,* 2 (1975), 50−60.

1496 REITER, R. E. "George Herbert and the Biographers." *Cithara,* 9, ii (1970), 18−31.

1497 RICKEY, M. E. "Rhymecraft in Edward and George Herbert." *JEGP,* 57 (1958), 502−11.

1498 RICKEY, M. E. "Herbert's Technical Development." *JEGP,* 62 (1963), 745−60.

1499 RICKEY, M. E. *Utmost Art: Complexity in the Verse of George Herbert.* Lexington: University of Kentucky Press, 1966.

1500 ROSS, M. M. "George Herbert and the Humanist Tradition." *UTQ,* 16 (1946−47), 169−82; and see **233.**

1501 RØSTVIG, M.-S. "Structural Images in Cowley and Herbert." *ES*, 54 (1973), 121 – 29.

1502 SANDLER, F. " 'Solomon Ubique Regnet': Herbert's Use of the Image of the New Covenant." *PLL*, 8 (1972), 147 – 58.

1503 SMITHSON, B. "Herbert's 'Affliction' Poems." *SEL*, 15 (1975), 125 – 40.

1504 STAMBLER, E. "The Unity of Herbert's *Temple*." *Cross Currents*, 10 (1960), 251 – 66.

1505 STANWOOD, P. G. "The Liveliness of Flesh and Blood: Herbert's 'Prayer I' and 'Love III.' " *SCN*, 31 (1973), 52 – 53.

1506 STEADMAN, J. M. "Herbert's Platonic Lapidary: A Note on 'The Foil.' " *SCN*, 30 (1972), 59 – 62.

1507 STEIN, A. "George Herbert's Prosody." *Lang&S*, 1 (1968), 1 – 38.

1508 STEIN, A. "George Herbert: The Art of Plainness." *The Poetic Tradition: Essays on Greek, Latin, and English Poetry*, ed. D. C. Allen and H. T. Rowell. Baltimore: Johns Hopkins Press, 1968.

1509 STEIN, A. *George Herbert's Lyrics*. Baltimore: Johns Hopkins Press, 1968.

1510 STEWART, S. "Time and *The Temple*." *SEL*, 6 (1966), 97 – 110.

1511 SUMMERS, J. H. *George Herbert: His Religion and Art*. Cambridge: Harvard University Press, 1954.

1512 SUMMERS, J. H. "Herbert's Form." *PMLA*, 66 (1951), 1055 – 72; and see **197** and **1511**.

1513 SUMMERS, J. H. "The Poem as Hieroglyph." See **196** and **1511**.

1514 TAYLOR, I. E. "Cavalier Sophistication in the Poetry of George Herbert." *ATR*, 39 (1957), 229 – 43.

1515 TAYLOR, M. *The Soul in Paraphrase: George Herbert's Poetics*. The Hague: Mouton, 1974.

1516 THOMPSON, E. N. S. "*The Temple* and *The Christian Year*." *PMLA*, 54 (1939), 1018 – 25.

1517 TUVE, R. "On Herbert's 'Sacrifice.' " *KR*, 12 (1950), 51 – 75.

1518 TUVE, R. *A Reading of George Herbert*. Chicago: University of Chicago Press, 1952.

1519 TUVE, R. "George Herbert and *Caritas*." *JWCI*, 22 (1959), 303 – 31; and *Essays by R. Tuve*, ed. T. P. Roche, Jr. Princeton: Princeton University Press, 1970.

1520 TUVE, R. "Sacred 'Parody' of Love Poetry, and Herbert." *SRen*, 8 (1961), 249 – 90; and *Essays by R. Tuve*, ed. T. P. Roche, Jr. Princeton: Princeton University Press, 1970.

1521 VENDLER, H. "The Re-invented Poem: George Herbert's Alternatives." *Forms of the Lyric*, . . . *English Institute*, ed. R. A. Brower. New York: Columbia University Press, 1970.

1522 VENDLER, H. "George Herbert's 'Vertue.' " *Ariel*, 1, ii (1970), 54 – 70.

1523 VENDLER, H. *The Poetry of George Herbert*. Cambridge: Harvard University Press, 1975.

1524 WALKER, J. D. "The Architectonics of George Herbert's *The Temple*." *ELH*, 29 (1962), 289 – 305.

1525 WALTON, I. "The Life of Mr. George Herbert." *English Biography in the Seventeenth Century,* ed. V. de Sola Pinto. London: Harrap, 1951. And see **2332** and **2340—43.**

1526 WARREN, A. "George Herbert." *Rage for Order: Essays in Criticism.* Chicago: University of Chicago Press, 1948.

1527 WATSON, G. "The Fabric of Herbert's *Temple.*" *JWCI,* 26 (1963), 354—58.

1528 WEST, M. "Ecclesiastical Controversy in George Herbert's 'Peace.' " *RES,* 22 (1971), 445—51.

1529 WHITE, H. C. "George Herbert. . . . " See **262.**

1530 WHITLOCK, B. W. "The Baroque Characteristics of the Poetry of George Herbert." *Cithara,* 7, ii (1968), 30—40.

1531 WICKES, G. "George Herbert's Views on Poetry." *RLV,* 21 (1955), 344—52.

1532 ZIEGELMAIER, G. "Liturgical Symbol and Reality in the Poetry of George Herbert." *American Benedictine Review,* 18 (1967), 344—53.

1533 ZITNER, S. P. "Herbert's 'Jordan' Poems." *Expl,* 9 (1950), Item 11.

Robert Herrick (1591— 1674)

Editions

1534 *Poetical Works,* ed. L. C. Martin. Oxford: Clarendon Press, 1956, 1963.

1535 *The Poetical Works,* ed. F. W. Moorman. London: Oxford University Press, 1915.

1536 *The Complete Poetry,* ed. J. M. Patrick. New York: New York University Press, 1963; Garden City: Doubleday, 1963; New York: Norton, 1968.

1537 *Selected Poems,* ed. J. Hayward. Baltimore: Penguin, 1961.

1538 [Selections], ed. H. N. Maclean. See **47.**

1539 [Selected Poetry,] ed. W. J. Smith. New York: Dell, 1962.

Bibliographies and Concordance

1540 GUFFEY, G. R., ed. *Robert Herrick, 1948— 1965. Elizabethan Bibliographies Supplements,* 3. London: Nether Press, 1968.

1541 HAGEMAN, E. H., ed. "Recent Studies in Herrick." *ELR,* 3 (1973), 462—71.

1542 MACLEOD, M. L., ed. *A Concordance to the Poems of Robert Herrick.* New York: Oxford University Press, 1936; New York: Haskell House, 1971.

Studies

1543 ALLEN, D. C. "Herrick's 'Rex Tragicus.' " *Studies in Honor of DeWitt T. Starnes*, ed. T. P. Harrison et al. Austin: University of Texas Press, 1967; and see **142.**

1544 BERMAN, R. "Herrick's Secular Poetry." *ES*, 52 (1971), 20−30; and see **47.**

1545 BROOKS, C. " 'Corinna's Going A-Maying.' " See **1065.**

1546 CAPWELL, R. L. "Herrick and the Aesthetic Principle of Variety and Contrast." *SAQ*, 71 (1972), 488−95.

1547 CHUTE, M. *Two Gentlemen: The Lives of George Herbert and Robert Herrick*. New York: Dutton, 1959.

1548 DELATTRE, F. *Robert Herrick: contribution a l'étude de la poésie lyrique en Angleterre au dix-septiéme siécle*. Paris: Alcan, 1912.

1549 DEMING, R. H. "Robert Herrick's Classical Ceremony." *ELH*, 34 (1967), 327−48.

1550 DEMING, R. H. "Herrick's Funereal Poems." *SEL*, 9 (1969), 153−67.

1551 DEMING, R. H. *Ceremony and Art: Robert Herrick's Poetry*. The Hague: Mouton, 1974.

1552 DENEEF, A. L. "Herrick and the Ceremony of Death." *RenP* (1970), 29−39.

1553 DENEEF, A. L. "Herrick's 'Corinna' and the Ceremonial Mode." *SAQ*, 70 (1971), 530−45.

1554 DENEEF, A. L. *"This Poetick Liturgie": Robert Herrick's Ceremonial Mode*. Durham: Duke University Press, 1974.

1555 GILBERT, A. H. "Robert Herrick on Death." *MLQ*, 5 (1944), 61−68.

1556 GODSHALK, W. L. "Art and Nature: Herrick and History." *EIC*, 17 (1967), 121−24.

1557 HIBBARD, G. R. "The Country House Poem." See **185.**

1558. HUGHES, R. E. "Herrick's 'Hock Cart': Companion Piece to 'Corinna's Going A-Maying.' " *CE*, 27 (1960), 420−22.

1559 JENKINS, P. R. "Rethinking What Moderation Means to Robert Herrick." *ELH*, 39 (1972), 49−65.

1560 KIMMEY, J. L. "Robert Herrick's Persona." *SP*, 67 (1970), 221−36.

1561 KIMMEY, J. L. "Robert Herrick's Satirical Epigrams." *ES*, 51 (1970), 312−23.

1562 KIMMEY, J. L. "Order and Form in Herrick's *Hesperides*." *JEGP*, 70 (1971), 255−68.

1563 LEAVIS, F. R. "Herrick." See **199.**

1564 LEITER, L. H. "Herrick's 'Upon Julia's Clothes.' " *MLN*, 73 (1958), 331.

1565 MANDEL, L. *Robert Herrick: The Last Elizabethan*. Chicago: University of Chicago Press, 1927.

1566 MOORMAN, F. W. *Robert Herrick: A Bibliographical and Critical Study*. New York: Lane, 1910, 1962.

1567 MUSGROVE, S. *The Universe of Robert Herrick*. Auckland: Auckland University College, 1950.

1568 PRESS, J. *Robert Herrick*. London: Longmans, Green, 1961.

1569 REA, J. "Persephone in 'Corinna's Going A-Maying.' " *CE*, 26 (1965), 44−46.

1570 REED, M. L. "Herrick Among the Maypoles: Dean Prior and the *Hesperides*." *SEL*, 5 (1965), 133−50.

1571 REGENOS, G. W. "The Influence of Horace on Robert Herrick." *PQ*, 26 (1947), 268−84.

1572 ROLLIN, R. B. *Robert Herrick*. New York: Twayne, 1966.

1573 ROSS, R. J. "Herrick's Julia in Silks." *EIC*, 15 (1965), 171−80.

1574 SCOTT, G. W. *Robert Herrick*. New York: St. Martin's, 1974.

1575 SHADOIAN, J. "Herrick's 'Delight in Disorder.' " *Studies in the Humanities*, 2 (1971), 23−25.

1576 SPITZER, L. "Herrick's 'Delight in Disorder.' " *MLN*, 76 (1961), 209−14.

1577 STARKMAN, M. K. " 'Noble Numbers' and the Poetry of Devotion." See **109.**

1578 STAUDT, V. P. "Horace and Herrick on *Carpe Diem*." *Classical Bulletin*, 33 (1957), 55−56.

1579 WENTERSDORF, K. P. "Herrick's Floral Imagery." *SN*, 36 (1964), 69−81.

1580 WHITAKER, T. R. "Herrick and the Fruits of the Garden." *ELH*, 22 (1955), 16−33.

1581 WITT, R. W. "Building a Pillar of Fame: [Herrick and Folklore]," *UMSE*, 13 (1972), 65−83.

1582 WOODWARD, D. H. "Herrick's Oberon Poems." *JEGP*, 64 (1965), 270−84.

Thomas Hobbes (1588– 1679)

Editions

1583 *The English Works of Thomas Hobbes*, ed. W. Molesworth. London: Bohn, 1839−45; Aalen: Scientia, 1962.

1584 *Selections*, ed. F. J. E. Woodbridge. New York: Scribner's, 1930.

1585 *Body, Man, and Citizen: Selections*, ed. R. S. Peters. New York: Collier, 1962.

1586 *Behemoth: The History of the Causes of the Civil Wars in England . . .*, ed. W. Molesworth. New York: Burt Franklin, 1963.

1587 *Behemoth; or, The Long Parliament*, ed. F. Tönnies. London: Simpkin, Marshall, 1889; second edition, New York: Barnes & Noble, 1969.

1588 *Elements of Law: Natural & Politic*, ed. F. Tönnies. Cambridge: Cambridge University Press, 1889, 1928; New York: Barnes & Noble, 1969.

1589 *De Cive or The Citizen*, ed. S. P. Lamprecht. New York: Appleton-Century-Crofts, 1949.

1590 *A Dialogue between a Philosopher and a Student of the Common Laws of England*, ed. J. Cropsey. Chicago: University of Chicago Press, 1971.

1591 *Leviathan*, ed. A. D. Lindsay. New York: Dutton, 1950, 1962.

1592 *Leviathan*, ed. C. B. Macpherson. Baltimore: Penguin, 1968.

1593 *Leviathan*, ed. M. Oakeshott. Oxford: Blackwell, 1947, 1957; New York: Collier, 1962.

1594 *Leviathan*, ed. J. Plamenatz. Cleveland: World Publishing, 1963.

1595 *Leviathan*, Parts 1 and 2, ed. H. W. Schneider. New York: Liberal Arts Press, 1958.

1596 *Leviathan*, ed. W. G. P. Smith. Oxford: Clarendon Press, 1909, 1962.

1597 *Leviathan*, ed. A. R. Waller. Cambridge: Cambridge University Press, 1904, 1935.

1598 *Man and Citizen. De homine*, trans. C. T. Wood, T. S. K. Scott-Craig, and B. Gert; *De cive*, trans. T. Hobbes; ed. B. Gert. Garden City: Doubleday, 1972.

1599 *Thuycides*, ed. D. Grene. Ann Arbor: University of Michigan Press, 1959.

Bibliography

1600 MACDONALD, H., and M. HARGREAVES, eds. *Thomas Hobbes: A Bibliography*. London: Bibliographical Society, 1952.

Studies

1601 ALEXANDER, R. W. "The Myth of Power: Hobbes's *Leviathan*." *JEGP*, 70 (1971), 31–50.

1602 BAUMRIN, B. H., ed. *Hobbes "Leviathan": Interpretation and Criticism*. Belmont: Wadsworth, 1969.

1603 BOND, D. F. "The Neo-classical Psychology of the Imagination." *ELH*, 4 (1937), 245–64.

1604 BOWLE, J. *Hobbes and his Critics: A Study in Seventeenth-Century Constitutionalism*. London: Cope, 1951.

1605 BRANDT, F. *Thomas Hobbes' Mechanical Conception of Nature*. Copenhagen: Levin & Munksgaard, 1928.

1606 BRETT, R. L. "Thomas Hobbes." *The English Mind*, ed. H. S. Davies and G. Watson. Cambridge: Cambridge University Press, 1964. *English Literature and British Philosophy*. Chicago: Chicago University Press, 1971.

1607 BROWN, K. C., ed. *Hobbes Studies*. Cambridge: Harvard University Press; Oxford: Blackwell, 1965.

1608 CHILD, A. "Making and Knowing in Hobbes, Vico, and Dewey." *University of California Publications in Philosophy*, No. 13. Berkeley: University of California Press, 1953.

1609 CRANSTON, M. W., and R. S. PETERS, eds. *Hobbes and Rousseau: A Collection of Critical Essays*. New York: Doubleday, 1972.

1610 GANG, T. M. "Hobbes and the Metaphysical Conceit—A Reply." *JHI*, 17 (1956), 418–21.

1611 GAUTHIER, D. P. *The Logic of "Leviathan": The Moral and Political Theory of Thomas Hobbes*. Oxford: Clarendon Press, 1969.

1612 GERT, B. "Hobbes and Psychological Egoism." *JHI*, 28 (1967), 503–20.

1613 GOLDSMITH, M. M. *Hobbes's Science of Politics*. New York: Columbia University Press, 1966.

1614 GREEN, A. W. "The Nature of Man and Personal Responsibility." *ModA*, 17 (1973), 183–94.

1615 HOOD, F. C. *The Divine Politics of Thomas Hobbes: An Interpretation of "Leviathan."* Oxford: Clarendon Press, 1964.

1616 JAMES, D. G. *The Life of Reason: Hobbes, Locke, Bolingbroke*. London: Longmans, Green, 1949.

1617 JESSOP, T. E. *Thomas Hobbes*. London, New York: Longmans, Green, 1961.

1618 KALLICH, M. "The Association of Ideas and Critical Theory: Hobbes, Locke, and Addison." *ELH*, 12 (1945), 290–315.

1619 KROOK, D. "Thomas Hobbes's Doctrine of Meaning and Truth." *Philosophy*, 31 (1956), 3–22.

1620 KROOK, D. *Three Traditions of Moral Thought*. Cambridge: Cambridge University Press, 1959.

1621 LAIRD, J. *Thomas Hobbes*. London: Benn, 1934; New York: Russell & Russell, 1968.

1622 LEVY, A. "The Economic Views of Thomas Hobbes." *JHI*, 15 (1954), 589–95.

1623 MacGILLIVRAY, R. "Thomas Hobbes's History of the English Civil War: A Study of *Behemoth*." *JHI*, 31 (1970), 179–98.

1624 MACPHERSON, C. B. *The Political Theory of Possessive Individualism: Hobbes to Locke*. Oxford: Clarendon Press, 1962.

1625 MAZZEO, J. A. "Hobbes: The Scientific Secularization of the World." See **111.**

1626 McNEILLY, F. S. *The Anatomy of "Leviathan."* New York: St. Martin's, 1967.

1627 MINTZ, S. I. *The Hunting of Leviathan: Seventeenth-Century Reactions to the Materialism and Moral Philosophy of Thomas Hobbes*. Cambridge: Cambridge University Press, 1962.

1628 NIGH, D. J. "Hobbes' Relevance to Dramatic Theory." *XUS*, 5 (1966), 153–63.

1629 PENNINGTON, D. H. "Political Debate and Thomas Hobbes." See 7.

1630 PETERS, R. *Hobbes.* Baltimore: Penguin, 1956.

1631 PINTO, V. de S. "Was Hobbes an Ogre?" *EIC,* 7 (1957), 22−27.

1632 RAPHAEL, D. D. "Rationalism in Hobbes's Political Philosophy." *Studies in Rationalism, Judaism, and Universalism,* ed. R. Loewe, New York: Humanities Press, 1967.

1633 ROBERTSON, D. B. "Hobbes's Theory of Associations in the Seventeenth-Century Milieu." *Voluntary Association: A Study of Groups in Free Association,* ed. D. B. Robertson. Richmond: John Knox Press, 1966.

1634 SELDEN, R. "Hobbes and Late Metaphysical Poetry." *JHI,* 35 (1974), 196−210.

1635 SPRAGENS, T. A., Jr. *The Politics of Motion: The World of Thomas Hobbes.* Lexington: University Press of Kentucky, 1973.

1636 STAUFFER, R. B., and W. E. VINACKE. "Hobbes Revisited: An Analysis of the Compatability of the Theories of Human Nature and of the State Found in *Leviathan.*" *JSP,* 48 (1958), 61 − 73.

1637 STEADMAN, J. M. "*Leviathan* and Renaissance Etymology." *JHI,* 28 (1967), 575−76.

1638 STEPHEN, L. *Hobbes.* London: Macmillan, 1904; Ann Arbor: University of Michigan Press, 1961.

1639 STEWART, J. B. "Hobbes Among the Critics." *Political Science Quarterly,* 73 (1958), 547−65.

1640 STRAUS, L. *The Political Philosophy of Hobbes.* Chicago: University of Chicago Press, 1952.

1641 TAYLOR, A. E. *Thomas Hobbes.* London: Constable, 1908; Port Washington: Kennikat, 1970.

1642 TAYLOR, A. E. "An Apology for Mr. Hobbes." See 123.

1643 THORPE, C. D. *The Aesthetic Theory of Thomas Hobbes.* Ann Arbor: University of Michigan Press, 1940; New York: Russell & Russell, 1964.

1644 WARRENDER, H. *The Political Philosophy of Hobbes: His Theory of Obligation.* Oxford: Clarendon Press, 1957.

1645 WARRENDER, H. "The Place of God in Hobbes's Philosophy." *Political Studies,* 8 (1960), 48−57.

1646 WATKINS, J. W. N. *Hobbes' System of Ideas: A Study in the Political Significance of Philosophical Theories.* London: Hutchinson, 1965.

1647 WATKINS, J. W. N. "The Posthumous Career of Thomas Hobbes." *RPol,* 19 (1957), 351−60.

1648 WATSON, G. "Hobbes and the Metaphysical Conceit." *JHI,* 16 (1955), 558−62.

1649 WILLEY, B. "The Philosophical Quest for Truth: Hobbes." See 136.

1650 WOODFIELD, R. "Hobbes on the Law of Nature and the Atheist." *RMS,* 15 (1971), 34−43.

James Howell (1593/94— 1666)

Editions

1651 *Epistolae Ho-Elianae,* ed. J. Jacobs. London: Nutt, 1890—92.

1652 *Epistolae Ho-Elianae,* ed. A. Repplier. Boston: Houghton-Mifflin, 1907.

1653 *Familiar Letters; or, Epistolae Ho-Elianae,* ed. O. Smeaton. London: Dent, 1903.

1654 *Epistolae Ho-Elianae,* ed. W. H. Bennett. London: Stott, 1890.

1655 *Certain Letters, Selected . . . ,* ed. R. J. Walsh. New York: Rudge, 1928.

1656 *Instructions for Forreine Travell,* ed. E. Arber. London: Constable, 1869; New York: AMS Press, 1966.

Studies

1657 BENSLY, E. "James Howell." *Aberystwyth Studies,* 3—6 (1922—24); 8—9, (1926—27).

1658 HIRST, V. M. "The Authenticity of James Howell's Familiar Letters." *MLR,* 54 (1959), 558—61.

1659 MENSEL, E. H. "James Howell as a Practical Theorist." *JEGP,* 25 (1926), 531—39.

1660 THOMPSON, E. N. S. "Familiar Letters." *Literary Bypaths of the Renaissance.* New Haven: Yale University Press, 1924; Freeport: Books for Libraries, 1968.

1661 VANN, W. H. *Notes on the Writings of James Howell.* Waco: Baylor University Press, 1924.

Ben Jonson (1572?— 1637)

Editions

1662 *Ben Jonson:* [*Works*], ed. C. H. Herford, P. and E. M. Simpson, 11 vols. Oxford: Clarendon Press, 1925—52.

1663 *Selected Works,* ed. H. Levin. New York: Random House, 1938.

1664 *Selected Works,* ed. D. McPherson. New York: Holt, Rinehart & Winston, 1972.

1665 *The Complete Poetry,* ed. W. B. Hunter, Jr. New York: New York University Press; Garden City: Doubleday, 1963; New York: Norton, 1968.

1666 *The Poems,* ed. B. H. Newdigate. Oxford: Blackwell, 1936.

1667 *Poems,* ed. G. B. Johnston. London: Routledge & Kegan Paul, 1954.

1668 *Selected Poetry,* ed. T. Gunn. Baltimore: Penguin, 1974.

1669 [Selected Poems], ed. J. Hollander. New York: Dell, 1961.

1670 [Selections], ed. H. N. Maclean. See **47.**

1671 *Literary Criticism,* ed. J. D. Redwine, Jr. Lincoln: University of Nebraska Press, 1969.

1672 *Conversations with William Drummond,* ed. R. F. Patterson. London: Blackie, 1923.

1673 *Discoveries, 1641; Conversations with William Drummond, 1619.* Edinburgh: Edinburgh University Press, 1923, 1966.

1674 *Timber, or Discoveries,* ed. I. Gollancz. London: Dent, 1951.

1675 *Discoveries, 1641; Conversations with William Drummond, 1619,* ed. G. B. Harrison. New York: Barnes & Noble, 1966.

1676 *Timber; or Discoveries,* ed. R. S. Walker. Syracuse: Syracuse University Press, 1953.

Bibliographies

1677 BROCK, D. H., and J. M. WELSH, eds. *Ben Jonson: A Quadricentennial Bibliography, 1947– 1972.* Metuchen: Scarecrow Press, 1974.

1678 GASTON, P. L. "Commendation and Approbation: Recent Ben Jonson Scholarship." *PLL,* 9 (1973), 423– 29.

1679 GUFFEY, G. R., ed. *Ben Jonson, 1945– 1965. Elizabethan Bibliographies Supplements,* 3. London: Nether Press, 1968.

1680 TANNENBAUM, S. A., ed. *A Concise Bibliography.* New York: Scholars' Facsimiles and Reprints, 1938; Supplement, 1947.

Comprehensive Studies

1681 ARNOLD, J. A *Grace Peculiar: Ben Jonson's Cavalier Heroes.* University Park: Pennsylvania State University Press, 1972.

1682 BAMBOROUGH, J. B. *Ben Jonson.* London, New York: Longmans, Green, 1959, 1965.

1683 BARISH, J. A., ed. *Ben Jonson: A Collection of Critical Essays.* Englewood Cliffs: Prentice-Hall, 1963.

1684 BEAURLINE, L. A. "The Selective Principle in Jonson's Shorter Poems." *Criticism* 8 (1966), 64– 74; and see **47.**

1685 BEAURLINE, L. A. "Ben Jonson and the Illusion of Completeness." *PMLA*, 84 (1969), 51−59.

1686 BLANSHARD, R. A. "Carew and Jonson." *SP*, 52 (1955), 195−211.

1687 BRADBROOK, F. W. "John Donne and Ben Jonson." *N&Q*, 202 (1957), 146−47.

1688 BRADBROOK, F. W. "Ben Jonson's Poetry." See 7.

1689 CHUTE, M. G. *Ben Jonson of Westminster*. New York: Dutton, 1953.

1690 COPE, J. I. "Jonson's Reading of Spenser: The Genesis of a Poem." *EM*, 10 (1959), 61−66.

1691 CUBETA, P. M. "Ben Jonson's Religious Lyrics." *JEGP*, 62 (1963), 96−110.

1692 DUNN, E. C. *Ben Jonson's Art: Elizabethan Life and Literature as Reflected Therein*. Northampton: Smith College, 1925.

1693 ELIOT, T. S. "Ben Jonson." See 86.

1694 EVANS, W. M. *Ben Jonson and Elizabethan Music*. Lancaster: Lancaster Press, 1929; New York: Da Capo, 1965.

1695 FRENCH, J. T. "Ben Jonson: His Aesthetic of Relief." *TSLL*, 10 (1968), 161−75.

1696 FRIEDBERG, H. "Ben Jonson's Poetry: Pastoral, Georgic, Epigram." *ELR*, 4 (1974), 111−36.

1697 GARDINER, J. K. "Line Counts, Word Counts, and Two Jonson Epistles." *Style*, 7 (1973), 30−38.

1698 GIANAKARIS, C. J. "The Humanism of Ben Jonson." *CLAJ*, 14 (1970), 115−26.

1699 GREENE, T. M. "Ben Jonson and the Centered Self." *SEL*, 10 (1970), 325−48.

1700 HILBERRY, C. B. *Ben Jonson's Ethics in Relation to Stoic and Humanist Thought*. Chicago: University of Chicago Press, 1933; Folcroft: Folcroft Library Editions, 1973.

1701 INGLIS, F. "Jonson the Master: Stones Well Squared." *The Elizabethan Poets*. London: Evans, 1969.

1702 JOHNSON, C. H. *Reason's Double Agent*. Chapel Hill: University of North Carolina Press, 1966.

1703 JOHNSTON, G. B. *Ben Jonson: Poet*. New York: Columbia University Press, 1945.

1704 KAY, W. D. "The Shaping of Ben Jonson's Career: A Reexamination of Facts and Problems." *MP*, 67 (1970), 224−37.

1705 KERRIGAN, W. "Ben Jonson Full of Shame and Scorn." *SLitI*, 6 (1973), 199−218.

1706 KNIGHTS, L. C. "Ben Jonson: Public Attitudes and Social Poetry." *A Celebration of Ben Jonson*, ed. W. Blissett et al. Toronto: University of Toronto Press, 1974.

1707 MACLEAN, H. N. "Ben Jonson's Poems: Notes on the Ordered Society." *Essays in English Literature from the Renaissance to the Victorian Age*, ed. M. MacLure and F. W. Watt. Toronto: University of Toronto Press, 1964; and see 47.

BEN JONSON

1708 MACLEAN, H. N. " 'A More Secret Cause': The Wit of Jonson's Poetry." *A Celebration of Ben Jonson*, ed. W. Blissett et al. Toronto: University of Toronto Press, 1974.

1709 MAROTTI, A. F. "All About Jonson's Poetry." *ELH*, 39 (1972), 208−37.

1710 McEUEN, K. A. *Classical Influences upon the Tribe of Ben: A Study of Classical Elements in the Non-dramatic Poetry of Ben Jonson and his Circle.* Cedar Rapids: Torch Press, 1939.

1711 MORTIMER, A. "The Feigned Commonwealth in the Poetry of Ben Jonson." *SEL*, 13 (1973), 69−79.

1712 NICHOLS, J. G. *The Poetry of Ben Jonson.* New York: Barnes & Noble, 1969.

1713 ORGEL, S. *The Jonsonian Masque.* Cambridge: Harvard University Press, 1965; and see **47**.

1714 PALMER, J. *Ben Jonson.* New York: Viking Press, 1934.

1715 PARFITT, G. A. E. "The Poetry of Ben Jonson." *EIC*, 18 (1968), 18−31.

1716 PARFITT, G. A. E. "Ethical Thought and Ben Jonson's Poetry." *SEL*, 9 (1969), 123−34; and see **47**.

1717 PARFITT, G. A. E. "Compromise Classicism: Language and Rhythm in Ben Jonson's Poetry." *SEL*, 11 (1971), 109−23.

1718 PASTER, G. K. "Ben Jonson and the Uses of Architecture." *RenQ*, 27 (1974), 306−20.

1719 PHELPS, G. "Ben Jonson's Poetry." See **7**.

1720 POTTS, L. J. "Ben Jonson and the Seventeenth Century." *ES*, 2 (1949), 7−24.

1721 SKELTON, R. "The Masterpoet and the Multiple Tradition: The Poetry of Ben Jonson." *Style*, 1 (1967), 225−46.

1722 SPANOS, W. V. "The Real Toad in the Jonsonian Garden: Resonance in the Non-dramatic Poetry." *JEGP*, 68 (1969), 1−23.

1723 SUMMERS, J. H. "The Heritage of Donne and Jonson." *UTQ*, 39 (1969−70), 107−26.

1724 TRIMPI, W. *Ben Jonson's Poems: A Study of the Plain Style.* Stanford: Stanford University Press, 1962.

1725 TRIMPI, W. "Jonson and the Neo-Latin Authorities for the Plain Style." *PMLA*, 77 (1962), 21−26.

1726 WALKER, R. S. "Ben Jonson's Lyric Poetry." *Criterion*, 13 (1933−34), 430−48; and see **196**.

1727 WALTON, G. "The Tone of Ben Jonson's Poetry." See **47**, **196**, and **255**.

1728 WHEELER, C. F. *Classical Mythology in the Plays, Masques, and Poems of Ben Jonson.* Princeton: Princeton University Press, 1938.

Studies: Poems

Miscellaneous

1729 BABB, H. S. "The 'Epitaph on Elizabeth, L. H.' and Ben Jonson's Style." *JEGP*, 62 (1963), 738–44.

1730 BROWN, A. D. F. " 'Drink to Me, Celia.' " *MLR*, 54 (1959), 554–57.

1731 CLUBB, R. L. "The Paradox of Ben Jonson's 'A Fit of Rime Against Rime.' " *CLAJ*, 5 (1961), 145–47.

1732 COMBELLACK, F. M. "Jonson's 'To John Donne.' " *Expl*, 17 (1958), Item 6.

1733 CUBETA, P. M. " 'A Celebration of Charis': An Evaluation of Jonson's Poetic Strategy." *ELH*, 25 (1958), 163–80.

1734 DONALDSON, I. "Jonson's Ode to Sir Lucius Cary and Sir H. Morison." *SLitI*, 6 (1973), 139–52.

1735 EVERETT, B. "Ben Jonson's 'A Vision of Beauty.' " *CritQ*, 1 (1959), 238–44.

1736 FIKE, F. "Ben Jonson's 'On My First Sonne.' " *GorR*, 11 (1969), 205–20.

1737 GARDINER, J. K. " 'To Heaven.' " *CP*, 6, ii (1973), 26–36.

1738 HELD, G. "Jonson's Pindaric on Friendship." *CP*, 3, i (1970), 29–41.

1739 HEMPHILL, G. "Jonson's *Fit of Rime against Rime*." *Expl*, 12 (1954), Item 50.

1740 HUTCHISON, B. "Ben Jonson's 'Let Me Be What I Am': An Apology in Disguise." *ELN*, 2 (1965), 185–90.

1741 JOHN, L. C. "Ben Jonson's 'To Sir William Sidney, On His Birthday.' " *MLR*, 52 (1957), 566–67.

1742 JONES, R. C. "The Satirist's Retirement in Jonson's 'Apologetical Dialogue.' " *ELH*, 34 (1967), 447–67.

1743 KAY, W. D. "The Christian Wisdom of Ben Jonson's 'On My First Sonne.' " *SEL*, 11 (1971), 125–36.

1744 MAY, L. F. "Jonson's 'Epitaph on Solomon Pavy.' " *Expl*, 20 (1961), Item 16.

1745 MEDINE, P. E. "Object and Intent in Jonson's 'Famous Voyage.' " *SEL*, 15 (1975), 97–110.

1746 PETERSON, R. S. "Virtue Reconciled to Pleasure: Jonson's 'A Celebration of Charis.' " *SLitI*, 6 (1973), 219–68.

1747 RACKIN, P. "Poetry Without Paradox: Jonson's 'Hymne' to Cynthia." *Criticism*, 4 (1962), 186–96.

1748 SYLVESTER, W. "Jonson's 'Come, My Celia' and Catullus' 'Carmen V.' " *Expl*, 12 (1964), Item 35.

1749 VAN DEUSEN, M. "Criticism and Ben Jonson's 'To Celia.' " *EIC*, 7 (1957), 95–103.

1750 WEINBERGER, G. J. "Jonson's Mock-Encomiastic 'Celebration of Charis.' " *Genre*, 4 (1971), 305–28.

Epigrams

1751 PARTRIDGE, E. "Jonson's *Epigrammes:* The Named and the Nameless." *SLitI*, 6 (1973), 153—98.

1752 PUTNEY, R. D. " 'This So Subtile Sport': Some Aspects of Jonson's Epigrams." *University of Colorado Studies,* 12, ed. J. K. Emery. Boulder: University of Colorado Press, 1966.

1753 SMITH, B. R. "Ben Jonson's *Epigrammes:* Portrait-Gallery, Theatre, Commonwealth." *SEL,* 14 (1974), 92—109.

1754 WYKES, D. "Ben Jonson's 'Chast Booke': *The Epigrammes.*" *RMS,* 13 (1969), 76—87.

To Penshurst

1755 CUBETA, P. M. "A Jonsonian Ideal: 'To Penshurst.' " *PQ,* 42 (1963), 14—24.

1756 DOUGLAS, J. W. " 'To Penshurst.' " *Christian Scholar.* 44 (1961), 133—38.

1757 HART, J. "Ben Jonson's Good Society: On the Growth of a Place and a Poem." *ModA,* 7 (1963), 61—68.

1758 HIBBARD, G. R. "The Country House Poem." See **185.**

1759 MOLESWORTH, C. " 'To Penshurst' and Jonson's Historical Imagination." *ClioW,* 1, ii (1972), 5—13.

1760 RATHMELL, J. C. A. "Jonson, Lord Lisle, and Penshurst." *ELR,* 1 (1971), 250—60.

1761 WILSON, G. A. "Jonson's Use of the Bible and the Great Chain of Being in 'To Penshurst.' " *SEL,* 8 (1968), 77—89.

Studies: Literary Theory

1762 BARKER, J. R. "A Pendant to Drummond of Hawthornden's *Conversations.*" *RES,* 16 (1965), 284—88.

1763 CALDER, D. G. "The Meaning of 'Imitation' in Jonson's *Discoveries.*" *NM,* 70 (1969), 435—40.

1764 FIELER, F. B. "The Impact of Bacon and the New Science Upon Jonson's Critical Thought in *Timber.*" *RenP* (1958—1960). Durham: Duke University Press, 1961.

1765 MACLEAN, H. N. "Ben Jonson's *Timber.* . . . " *PLL,* 10 (1974), 202—6.

1766 PEBWORTH, T.-L. "Jonson's *Timber* and the Essay Tradition." *Essays in Honor of E. L. Marilla,* ed. T. A. Kirby and W. J. Olive. Baton Rouge: Louisiana State University Press, 1971.

1767 STAINER, C. L. *Jonson and Drummond, Their Conversations.* Oxford: Blackwell, 1925.

1768 WALKER, R. S. "Literary Criticism in Jonson's Conversations with Drummond." *English*, 8 (1951), 222 – 30.

1769 WALKER, R. S. "Ben Jonson's Discoveries: A New New Analysis." *E&S*, 5 (1952), 32 – 42.

Henry King (1592 – 1669)

Editions

1770 *Poems*, ed. J. R. Baker. Denver: Swallow, 1960.

1771 *Poems*, ed. M. Crum. Oxford: Clarendon Press, 1965.

1772 *Poems*, ed. L. Mason. New Haven: Yale University Press, 1914.

1773 *The Poems*, ed. J. Sparrow. London: Nonesuch, 1925; Folcroft: Folcroft Library Editions, 1973.

Bibliographies

1774 BERRY, L. E., ed. "Henry King: [Bibliography]." See **4**.

1775 SPENCER, T., ed. "Henry King: [Bibliography]." See **17**.

Studies

1776 BERMAN, R. *Henry King and the Seventeenth Century*. London: Chatto & Windus, 1964.

1777 GLECKNER, R. F. "Henry King: A Poet of His Age." *Transactions of the Wisconsin Academy of Sciences, Arts, and Letters*, 65 (1956), 149 – 67.

1778 GLECKNER, R. F. "King's *The Exequy*." *Expl*, 12 (1954), Item 46.

1779 HAMMOND, G. *The Poetry of Bishop Henry King*. Boulder: University of Colorado Press, 1945.

1780 LOW, A. "A Metrical Device in 'The Exequy.' " *MLR*, 63 (1968), 7 – 12.

1781 MASON, L. "The Life and Works of Henry King." *Transactions of the Connecticut Academy of Arts and Sciences*, 18 (1913), 225 – 89.

Francis Kynaston (1587—1642)

Edition

1782 *Minor Poets of the Caroline Period,* ed. G. Saintsbury. Vol II. Oxford: Clarendon Press, 1906.

Studies

1783 HIGGINS, A. I. T. *Secular Heroic Poetry of the Caroline Period.* Bern: Francke, 1953.

1784 PERKINSON, R. H. "The Epic in Five Acts." *SP,* 43 (1946), 465—81.

1785 SECCOMBE, H. G. "Notes on Sir Francis Kynaston." *RES,* 8 (1932), 311—12.

1786 TURNBULL, G. H. "Samuel Hartlib's Connection with Kynaston's Musaeum Minervae." *N&Q,* 197 (1952).

Richard Lovelace (1618—1657)

Editions

1787 *The Poems,* ed. C. H. Wilkinson. Oxford: Clarendon Press, 1925, 1953.

1788 *Minor Poets of the Seventeenth Century,* ed. R. G. Howarth. New York: Dutton, 1931.

1789 [Selections], ed. H. N. Maclean. See **47.**

Studies

1790 ALLEN, D. C. "Richard Lovelace: 'The Grasse-Hopper.' " See **47, 142,** and **196.**

1791 ANSELMENT, R. A. " 'Griefe Triumphant' and 'Victorious Sorrow': A Reading of Richard Lovelace's 'The Falcon.' " *JEGP,* 70 (1971), 404—17.

1792 BERRY, H., and E. K. TIMINGS. "Lovelace at Court and a Version of Part of His 'The Scrutinie.' " *MLN,* 69 (1954), 167—70.

1793 EVANS, W. M. "Lawes' and Lovelace's 'Loose Saraband.' " *PMLA,* 54 (1939), 764—67.

1794 EVANS, W. M. "Richard Lovelace's 'Mock-Song.' " *PQ,* 24 (1945), 317−28.

1795 EVANS, W. M. "Lovelace's Concept of Prison Life in *The Vintage to the Dungeon.*" *PQ,* 26 (1947), 62−68.

1796 HARTMANN, C. H. *The Cavalier Spirit and its Influence in the Life and Work of Richard Lovelace.* New York: Dutton, 1925; New York: Haskell House, 1973.

1797 JONES, G. F. " 'Lov'd I Not Honour More': The Durability of a Literary Motif." *CL,* 11 (1959), 131−43.

1798 KING, B. "Green Ice and a Breast of Proof." *CE,* 26 (1965), 511−15.

1799 KING, B. "*The Grasse-hopper* and Allegory." *Ariel E,* 1, ii (1970), 71−82.

1799a MINER, E. *The Cavalier Mode.* See **216.**

1800 PEARSON, N. H. "Lovelace's *To Lucasta, Going to the Warres.*" *Expl,* 7 (1949), Item 58.

1801 SCOULAR, K. W. "Richard Lovelace. . . . " See **235.**

1802 SKELTON, R. *The Cavalier Poets.* See **240.**

1803 WADSWORTH, R. L., Jr. "On 'The Snayle' by Richard Lovelace." *MLR,* 65 (1970), 750−60.

1804 WALTON, G. "The Cavalier Poets." See **7.**

1805 WEDGWOOD, C. V. "Cavalier Poetry and Cavalier Politics." *Velvet Studies.* London: Cape, 1946.

1806 WEIDHORN, M. *Richard Lovelace.* New York: Twayne, 1970.

1807 WILLIAMSON, C. F. "Two Notes on the Poems of Lovelace." *MLR,* 52 (1957), 227−29.

Andrew Marvell (1621− 1678)

Editions

1808 *The Complete Works,* ed. A. B. Grosart. London: Robson, 1872−75; New York: AMS Press, 1966.

1809 *The Poems and Letters,* ed. H. M. Margoliouth; revised by P. Legouis. New York: Oxford University Press, 1971.

1810 *The Complete Poems,* ed. E. Donno. Baltimore: Penguin, 1972; New York: St. Martin's, 1974.

1811 *The Complete Poetry,* ed. G. de F. Lord. New York: Random House, 1968.

1812 *The Poems,* ed. H. Macdonald. Cambridge: Harvard University Press, 1952.

1813 *The Poems,* ed. J. Reeves and M. Seymour-Smith. New York: Barnes & Noble, 1969.

1814 *Selected Poetry and Prose,* ed. D. Davison. London: Harrap, 1952.

1815 *Selected Poetry,* ed. F. Kermode. Bergenfield: New American Library, 1967.

1816 [Selected Poetry], ed. J. H. Summers. New York: Dell, 1961.

1817 *The Latin Poetry,* ed. W. A. McQueen and K. A. Rockwell. Chapel Hill: University of North Carolina Press, 1964.

1818 *The Rehearsal Transpros'd,* ed. D. I. B. Smith. New York: Oxford University Press, 1971.

Bibliographies and Concordance

1819 BERRY, L. E., ed. "Andrew Marvell: [Bibliography]." See **4**.

1820 DONOVAN, D. G., ed. *Andrew Marvell, 1927– 1967. Elizabethan Bibliographies Supplements,* 12. London: Nether Press, 1969.

1821 GUFFEY, G. R., ed. *A Concordance to the English Poetry of Andrew Marvell.* Chapel Hill: University of North Carolina Press, 1974.

1822 SMITH, D. I. B., ed. "Marvell, 1621 – 1678: [Bibliography]." See **6**.

1823 SPENCER, T., ed. "Andrew Marvell: [Bibliography]." See **17**.

1824 SZANTO, G., ed. "Recent Studies in Marvell." *ELR,* 5 (1975), 273 – 86.

Comprehensive Studies

1825 ALVAREZ, A. "Marvell and the Poetry of Judgment." *HudRev,* 13 (1960), 417 – 28; and see **1899**.

1826 ANSELMENT, R. A. "Satiric Strategy in Marvell's *The Rehearsal Transpros'd." MP,* 68 (1970), 137 – 50.

1827 ANSELMENT, R. A. " 'Betwixt Jest and Earnest': Ironic Reversal in Andrew Marvell's *The Rehearsal Transpros'd." MLR,* 66 (1971), 282 – 93.

1828 BAIN, C. E. "The Latin Poetry of Andrew Marvell." *PQ,* 38 (1959), 436 – 49.

1829 BENNETT, J. "Andrew Marvell." See **148**.

1830 BEREK, P. "The Voices of Marvell's Lyrics." *MLQ,* 32 (1971), 143 – 57.

1831 BERTHOFF, A. E. *The Resolved Soul: A Study of Marvell's Major Poems.* Princeton: Princeton University Press, 1970.

1832 BRADBROOK, F. W. "The Poetry of Andrew Marvell." See **7**.

1833 BRADBROOK, M. C., and M. G. L. THOMAS. *Andrew Marvell.* Cambridge: Cambridge University Press, 1940, 1961.

1834 BRADBROOK, M. C. "Marvell and the Poetry of Rural Solitude." *RES,* 17 (1941), 37 – 46.

1835 CAREY, J., ed. *Andrew Marvell: A Critical Anthology.* Baltimore: Penguin, 1969.

1836 CARPENTER, M. "From Herbert to Marvell: Poetics in 'A Wreath' and 'The Coronet.' " *JEGP,* 69 (1970), 155 – 69.

1837 CARSCALLEN, J. "Marvell's Infinite Parallels." *UTQ*, 39 (1969–70), 144–63.

1838 CHAMBERS, A. B. " 'I was But an Inverted Tree': Notes Toward the History of an Idea." *SRen*, 8 (1961), 291–99.

1839 CHERNAIK, W. L. "Politics and Literature in Marvell." *RES*, 16 (1972), 25–36.

1840 COLIE, R. L. *"My Echoing Song:"Andrew Marvell's Poetry of Criticism.* Princeton: Princeton University Press, 1970.

1841 COOLIDGE, J. S. "Martin Marprelate, Marvell, and *Decorum Personae* as a Satirical Theme." *PMLA*, 74 (1959), 526–32.

1842 COOLIDGE, J. S. "Marvell and Horace." *MP*, 63 (1965), 111–20; and see **1866.**

1843 CORDER, J. "Marvell and Nature." *N&Q*, 6 (1959), 58–61.

1844 CREASER, J. "Marvell's Effortless Superiority." *EIC*, 20 (1970), 403–24.

1845 CULLEN, P. S. *Spenser, Marvell and Renaissance Pastoral.* Cambridge: Harvard University Press, 1970.

1846 DATTA, K. S. "Marvell and Wotton: A Reconsideration." *RES*, 19 (1968), 403–5.

1847 DAVISON, D. *The Poetry of Andrew Marvell.* London: Arnold; Great Neck: Barron's, 1964.

1848 DORENKAMP, A. G. "Marvell's Geometry of Love." *ELN*, 9 (1971), 111–15.

1849 ELIOT, T. S. "Andrew Marvell." See **86, 1835, 1866,** and **1899.**

1850 FRIEDMAN, D. M. *Marvell's Pastoral Art.* Berkeley: University of California Press, 1970.

1851 GOMME, A. "The Teasingness of Andrew Marvell." *OR*, 8 (1968), 13–33; 9 (1969), 49–73.

1852 GRANSDEN, K. W. "Time, Guilt, and Pleasure: A Note on Marvell's Nostalgia." *ArielE*, 1, ii (1970), 83–97.

1853 HALEWOOD, W. H. "Marvell. . . : The Psalm Model of Reconciliation." See **180.**

1854 HARTMAN, G. H. "Marvell, St. Paul, and the Body of Hope." *ELH*, 31 (1964), 175–94; and see **1866.**

1855 HILL, C. "Andrew Marvell and the Good Old Cause." *Mainstream*, 12 (1959), 1–27.

1856 HODGE, R. I. V. "Marvell's Fairfax Poems: Some Considerations Concerning Dates." *MP*, 71 (1973–74), 347–55.

1857 HYMAN, L. W. " 'Ideas' in Marvell's Poetry." *HINL*, 2 (1956), 29–31.

1858 HYMAN, L. W. "Politics and Poetry in Andrew Marvell." *PMLA*, 73 (1958), 475–79.

1859 HYMAN, L. W. *Andrew Marvell.* New York: Twayne, 1964.

1860 KALSTONE, D. "Marvell and the Fictions of Pastoral." *ELR*, 4 (1974), 174–88.

1861 LEGOUIS, P. *Andrew Marvell, Poet, Puritan, Patriot.* Oxford: Clarendon Press, 1965.

1862 LEISHMAN, J. B. *The Art of Marvell's Poetry*. London: Hutchinson, 1966; New York: Funk & Wagnalls, 1968.

1863 LEISHMAN, J. B. "Some Themes and Variations in the Poetry of Andrew Marvell." *PBA*, 47 (1961), 223–41; and see **1899**.

1864 LERNER, L. D. "Pastoral v. Christianity: Nature in Marvell." *Seven Studies in English*, ed. G. Roberts. London: Parnell, 1971.

1865 LORD, G. de F. "From Contemplation to Action: Marvell's Poetical Career." *PQ*, 46 (1967), 207–24; and see **1866**.

1866 LORD, G. de F., ed. *Andrew Marvell: A Collection of Critical Essays*. Englewood Cliffs: Prentice-Hall, 1968.

1867 MacCAFFREY, I. "Some Notes on Marvell's Poetry, Suggested by a Reading of His Prose." *MP*, 61 (1964), 261–69.

1868 MARTZ, L. L. "Andrew Marvell: The Mind's Happiness." See **209**.

1869 MINER, E. *The Metaphysical Mode*. See **215**.

1870 MORGAN, D. "The Occasion for Marvell's *Growth of Popery*." *JHI*, 21 (1960), 568–70.

1871 MORRIS, B. "Satire from Donne to Marvell." See **218**.

1872 NEVO, R. Marvell's 'Songs of Innocence and Experience.' " *SEL*, 5 (1965), 1–21.

1873 NORFORD, D. P. "Marvell and the Arts of Contemplation and Action." *ELH*, 41 (1974), 50–73.

1874 PITMAN, M. R. "Andrew Marvell and Sir Henry Wotton." *RES*, 13 (1962), 157–58.

1875 PRESS, J. *Andrew Marvell*. London: Longmans, Green, 1958; revised edition, 1966.

1876 QUIVEY, J. "Rhetoric and Frame: A Study of Method in Three Satires by Marvell." *TSL*, 18 (1973), 75–91.

1877 ROBBINS, C. "Marvell's Religion: Was He a New Methodist?" *JHI*, 23 (1962), 268–72.

1878 ROSENBERG, J. D. "Marvell and the Christian Idiom." *BUSE*, 4 (1960), 152–61.

1879 SALERNO, N. A. "Andrew Marvell and the Grafter's Art." *EA*, 11 (1968), 151–60.

1880 SALERNO, N. A. "Andrew Marvell and the *Furor Hortensis*." *SEL*, 8 (1968), 103–20.

1881 SICHERMAN, C. M. "The Mocking Voices of Donne and Marvell." *BuR*, 17, ii (1969), 32–46.

1882 SMITH, D. I. B. "The Political Beliefs of Andrew Marvell." *UTQ*, 36 (1966–67), 55–67.

1883 SMITH, D. I. B. "Editing Marvell's Prose." See **283**.

1884 SPENCER, J. B. *Hervic Nature: . . . from Marvell to Thomson*. See **244**.

1885 SPITZ, L. "Process and Stasis: Aspects of Nature in Vaughan and Marvell." *HLQ*, 5 (1969), 415–22.

1886 STEWART, S. "Marvell and the *Ars Moriendi*." See **114**.

1887 SUMMERS, J. H. "Marvell's 'Nature.' " *ELH,* 20 (1953), 121 – 35; and see **1835, 1866,** and **1899.**

1888 SUMMERS, J. H. "Andrew Marvell: Private Taste and Public Judgement." *Stratford-upon-Avon Studies,* 11 (1970), 181 – 210; and see **246.**

1889 SUTHERLAND, J. R. "A Note on the Satirical Poetry of Andrew Marvell." *PQ,* 45 (1966), 46 – 53.

1891 TAYLER, E. W. "Marvell's Garden of the Mind." See **129** and **1899.**

1892 TOLIVER, H. E. "Pastoral Form and Idea in Some Poems of Marvell." *TSLL,* 5 (1963), 83 – 97.

1893 TOLIVER, H. E. *Marvell's Ironic Vision.* New Haven: Yale University Press, 1965.

1894 VARMA, R. S. *Imagery and Thought . . . .* See **250.**

1895 WALLACE, J. M. *Destiny His Choice: The Loyalism of Andrew Marvell.* Cambridge: Cambridge University Press, 1968.

1896 WALLERSTEIN, R. C. "Marvell and the Various Light." See **254.**

1897 WARNKE, F. J. "Play and Metamorphosis in Marvell's Poetry." *SEL,* 5 (1965), 23 – 30.

1898 WILCHER, R. "Marvell's Cherry: A Reply to Mr. Salerno." *EA,* 23 (1970), 406 – 9.

1899 WILDING, M. *Marvell: Modern Judgements.* London: Macmillan, 1969.

Studies: Poems

Miscellaneous

1900 BATESON, F. W., and F. R. LEAVIS. " 'A Dialogue between the Soul and Body': A Debate." See **1899.**

1901 BERTHOFF, A. E. "The Allegorical Metaphor: Marvell's 'The Definition of Love.' " *RES,* 17 (1966), 77 – 84.

1902 BERTHOFF, A. E. "The Voice of Allegory: Marvell's 'The Unfortunate Lover.' " *MLQ,* 27 (1966), 41 – 50.

1903 CALDERWOOD, J. L. "Marvell's 'The Coronet.' " *EngR,* 15 (1965), 18 – 19.

1904 DATTA, K. S. "New Light on Marvell's 'A Dialogue Between the Soul and Body.' " *RenQ,* 22 (1969), 242 – 55.

1905 DAVISON, D. "Marvell's 'The Definition of Love.' " *RES,* 6 (1955), 141 – 46.

1906 DUNCAN-JONES, E. E. "A Reading of Marvell's 'The Unfortunate Lover.' " *I. A. Richards: Essays in His Honor,* ed. R. Brower et al. New York: Oxford University Press, 1973.

1907 EVERETT, B. "Marvell's 'The Mower's Song.' " *CritQ,* 4 (1962), 219 – 24.

1908 FISHER, A. S. "The Augustan Marvell: 'The Last Instructions to a Painter.' " *ELH,* 38 (1971), 223 – 38.

1909 GEARIN-TOSH, M. "The Structure of Marvell's 'Last Instructions to a Painter.' " *EIC*, 22 (1972), 48−57.

1910 GOLDBERG, J. S. "The Typology of 'Musicks Empire.' " *TSLL*, 13 (1971), 421−30.

1911 HARDY, J. E. "Andrew Marvell's 'The Coronet': The Frame of Curiosity." *The Curious Frame*. Notre Dame: University of Notre Dame Press, 1962. And see **1899.**

1912 HINNANT, C. H. "Marvell's Gallery of Art." *RenQ*, 24 (1971), 26−37.

1913 KERMODE, F. "The Banquet of Sense." *BJRL*, 44 (1961), 68−99.

1914 KERMODE, F. "The Definitions of Love." *RES*, 7 (1956), 183−85.

1915 KING, B. " 'The Mower against Gardens' and the Levellers." *HLQ*, 33 (1970), 237−42.

1916 KING, B. "A Reading of Marvell's 'The Coronet.' " *MLR*, 68 (1973), 741−49.

1917 MINER, E. "The 'Poetic Picture, Painted Poetry' of *The Last Instructions to a Painter.*" *MP*, 63 (1966), 288−94; and see **1866.**

1918 PATRICK, J. M. "Marvell's *The Unfortunate Lover.*" *Expl*, 20 (1962), Item 65.

1919 ROSA, A. F. "Andrew Marvell's 'On a Drop of Dew': A Reading and a Possible Source." *CP*, 5, i (1972), 57−59.

1920 SAVESON, J. E. "Marvell's 'On a Drop of Dew.' " *N&Q*, 5 (1958), 289-90.

1921 SCHULZE, E. J. "The Reach of Wit: Marvell's 'The Definition of Love.' " *PMASAL*, 50 (1965), 563−74.

1922 SCHWENGER, P. T. "Marvell's 'Unfortunate Lover' as Device." *MLQ*, 35 (1974), 364−75.

1923 TOLIVER, H. E. "The Strategy of Marvell's Resolve Against Created Pleasure." *SEL*, 4 (1964), 57−69.

1924 TOLIVER, H. E. "Marvell's 'The Definition of Love' and Poetry of Self-Expression." *BuR*, 10 (1965), 263−74; and see **1866.**

1925 WILSON, A. J. N. "Andrew Marvell: *Upon the Hill and Grove at Bill-Borow* and *Musicks Empire.*" *BJRL*, 51 (1969), 453−82.

Bermudas

1926 BENJAMIN, E. B. "Marvell's *Bermudas.*" *CEA*, 30, vii (1967), 10−12.

1927 COLIE, R. L. "Marvell's 'Bermudas' and the Puritan Paradise." *RN*, 10 (1957), 75−79.

1928 CUMMINGS, R. M. "The Difficulty of Marvell's 'Bermudas.' " *MP*, 67 (1970), 331−40.

1929 WILDING, M. " 'Apples' in Marvell's 'Bermudas.' " *ELN*, 6 (1969), 254−57.

The Garden

1930 BERGER, H., Jr. "Marvell's 'Garden': Still Another Interpretation." *MLQ*, 28 (1967), 285 – 304.

1931 CALHOUN, T. O., and J. M. POTTER. *Marvell's "The Garden": A Casebook.* Columbus: Merrill, 1970.

1932 CARPENTER, M. "Marvell's 'Garden.' " *SEL*, 10 (1970), 155 – 69.

1933 EMPSON, W. "Marvell's Garden." See **172** and **1899.**

1934 GODSHALK, W. L. "Marvell's Garden and the Theologians." *SP*, 66 (1969), 639 – 53.

1935 HENSLEY, C. S. "Thomas Wilson's *Christian Dictionary* and the 'Idea' of Marvell's 'Garden.' " *New Aspects of Lexicography, Literary Criticism.* Carbondale: Southern Illinois University Press, 1972.

1936 HYMAN, L. W. "Marvell's 'Garden.' " *ELH*, 25 (1958), 13 – 22.

1937 KERMODE, F. "The Argument of Marvell's 'Garden.' " *EIC*, 2 (1952), 225 – 41; and see **196, 1835,** and **1899.**

1938 POGGIOLI, R. "Work in Progress: The Pastoral of the Self." *Daedalus*, 88 (1959), 686 – 99.

1939 POTTER, J. M. "Another Porker in the Garden of Epicurus: Marvell's 'Hortus' and 'The Garden.' " *SEL*, 11 (1971), 137 – 51.

1940 RØSTVIG, M.-S. "Andrew Marvell's 'The Garden': A Hermetic Poem." *ES*, 40 (1959), 65 – 76.

1941 RØSTVIG, M.-S. *The Happy Man.* See **320.**

1942 SERIO, J. N. "Andrew Marvell's 'The Garden': An Anagogic Reading." *OUR*, 12 (1970), 68 – 76.

1943 SIEMON, J. E. "Generic Limits in Marvell's 'Garden.' " *PLL*, 8 (1972), 261 – 72.

1944 STEMPEL, D. " 'The Garden': Marvell's Cartesian Ecstasy." *JHI*, 28 (1967), 99 – 114.

1945 STEWART, S. *The Enclosed Garden.* See **245.**

1946 SUMMERS, J. H. "Reading Marvell's 'Garden.' " *CentR*, 13 (1969), 18 – 37.

1947 WILLIAMSON, J. "The Context of Marvell's 'Hortus' and 'Garden.' " *MLN*, 76 (1961), 590 – 98; and see **139.**

The Nymph Complaining

1948 ALLEN, D. C. "Andrew Marvell: 'The Nymph Complaining for the Death of her Fawn.' " See **142.**

1949 EMERSON, E. H. "Andrew Marvell's *The Nymph Complaining for the Death of her Faun.*" *EA*, 8 (1955), 107 – 10.

1950 GUILD, N. "Marvell's 'The Nymph Complaining for the Death of Her Faun.' " *MLQ*, 29 (1968), 385 – 94.

1951 HARTMAN, G. H. " 'The Nymph Complaining for the Death of Her Fawn': A Brief Allegory." *EIC*, 18 (1968), 131 – 35.

1952 LE COMTE, E. S. "Marvell's 'The Nymph Complaining for the Death of Her Fawn.' " *MP*, 50 (1952), 97 – 101; and see **200** and **1835**.

1953 LEGOUIS, P. "Marvell's 'Nymph Complaining for the Death of Her Faun': *A mise au point*." *MLQ*, 21 (1960), 30 – 32.

1954 MINER, E. "The Death of Innocense in Marvell's 'Nymph Complaining for the Death of her Faun.' " *MP*, 65 (1967), 9 – 16; and see **215** and **1899**.

1955 REESE, J. E. "Marvell's *Nymph* in a New Light." *EA* (1965), 398 – 401.

1956 SPITZER, L. "Marvell's 'Nymph Complaining for the Death of Her Faun': Sources versus Meaning." *MLQ*, 19 (1958), 231 – 43; and see **196**.

1957 WILLIAMSON, K. "Marvell's 'The Nymph': . . . A Reply." *MP*, 51 (1954), 268 – 71.

To His Coy Mistress

1959 CARROLL, J. J. "The Sun and the Lovers in 'To His Coy Mistress.' " *MLN*, 74 (1959), 4 – 7.

1960 CUNNINGHAM, J. V. "Logic and Lyric." *MP*, 51 (1953), 33 – 41; and see **161** and **1899**.

1961 DATTA, K. S. "Marvell's Stork: The Natural History of an Emblem." *JWCI*, 31 (1968), 437 – 38.

1962 DAVISON, D. "Notes on Marvell's 'To His Coy Mistress.' " *N&Q*, 5 (1958), 521.

1963 FARNHAM, A. E. "Saint Teresa and the Coy Mistress." *BUSE*, 2 (1956), 226 – 39.

1964 GWYNN, F. L. "Marvell's *To His Coy Mistress*, 33 – 46." *Expl*, 11 (1953), Item 49.

1965 HARTWIG, J. "The Principle of Measure in 'To His Coy Mistress.' " *CE*, 25 (1964), 572 – 75.

1966 HOGAN, P. G., Jr. "Marvell's 'Vegetable Love.' " *SP*, 60 (1963), 1 – 11.

1967 HYMAN, L. W. "Marvell's 'Coy Mistress' and Desperate Lover." *MLN*, 75 (1960), 8 – 10.

1968 KING, B. "Irony in Marvell's 'To His Coy Mistress.' " *SoR*, 5 (1969), 689 – 703.

1969 LOW, A., and P. J. PIVAL. "Rhetorical Pattern in Marvell's 'To His Coy Mistress.' " *JEGP*, 68 (1969), 414 – 21.

1970 MILLER, B. E. "Logic in Marvell's 'To His Coy Mistress.' " *NDQ*, 30 (1962), 48 – 49.

1971 MOLDENHAUER, J. J. "The Voices of Seduction in 'To His Coy Mstress': A Rhetorical Analysis." *TSLL*, 10 (1968), 189 – 206.

1972 OWER, J. "Spatial Symbolism in Marvell's 'To His Coy Mistress.' " *LURev*, 3 (1970), 25 – 35.

1973 PUTNEY, R. " 'Our Vegetable Love': Marvell and Burton." See **68.**

1974 ROLLIN, R. B. "Images of Libertinism in *Every Man in His Humor* and 'To His Coy Mistress.' " *PLL,* 6 (1970), 188—91.

1975 SASEK, L. A. "Marvell's 'To His Coy Mistress.' " *Expl,* 14 (1956), Item 47.

1976 SEDELOW, W. A., Jr. "Marvell's *To His Coy Mistress.*" *MLN,* 71 (1956), 6—8.

1977 WHEATCROFT, J. "Andrew Marvell and the Winged Chariot." *BuR,* 6, iii (1956), 22—53.

Upon Appleton House

1978 ALLEN, D. C. "Andrew Marvell: 'Upon Appleton House.' " See **142.**

1979 BERGER, H., Jr. "Marvell's 'Upon Appleton House': An Interpretation." *SoRA,* 1 (1965), 7—32.

1980 EVETT, D. " 'Paradice's Only Map': The *Topos* of the *Locus Amoenus* and the Structure of Marvell's *Upon Appleton House.*" *PMLA,* 85 (1970), 504—13.

1981 LEGOUIS, P. "Marvell's Grasshoppers." *N&Q,* 5 (1958), 108—9.

1982 MOLESWORTH, C. "Marvell's 'Upon Appleton House': The Persona as Historian, Philosopher, and Priest." *SEL,* 13 (1973), 149—62.

1983 O'LOUGHLIN, M. J. K. "This Sober Frame: A Reading of 'Upon Appleton House.' " See **1866.**

1984 RICHMOND, H. M. "Rural Lyricism: A Renaissance Mutation of the Pastoral." *CL,* 16 (1964), 193—210.

1985 RØSTVIG, M.-S. " 'Upon Appleton House' and the Universal History of Man." *ES,* 42 (1961), 337—51; and see **320** and **1899.**

1986 ROTH, F. H., Jr. "Marvell's 'Upon Appleton House': A Study in Perspective." *TSLL,* 14 (1972), 269—81.

1987 SCOULAR, K. W. "Andrew Marvell: 'Upon Appleton House. . . . ' " See **235.**

Poems on Cromwell

1988 BARON, H. "Marvell's 'Horatian Ode' and Machiavelli." *JHI,* 21 (1960), 450—51.

1989 BROOKS, C. "Criticism and Literary History: Marvell's 'Horatian Ode.' " *SR,* 55 (1947), 199—222; *English Institute Essays* (1946); New York: Columbia University Press, 1947; and see **196, 1833,** and **1899.**

1990 BROOKS, C. "A Note on the Limits of 'History' and the Limits of 'Criticism' [and Marvell's *Horatian Ode*]." *SR,* 61 (1953), 129—35; and see **196.**

1991 BUSH, D. "Marvell's 'Horatian Ode.' " *SR,* 60 (1952), 363—76, and see **196, 1833,** and **1899.**

1992 CARENS, J. F. "Andrew Marvell's Cromwell Poems." *BuR*, 7, i (1957), 41−70.

1993 DUNCAN-JONES, E. E. "The Erect Sword in Marvell's 'Horatian Ode.' " *EA*, 15 (1962), 172−74.

1994 EDWARDS, T. R. "*An Horatian Ode:* The Art of Power." See **167.**

1995 GARDNER, C. O. "Another View of Marvell's *Horatian Ode.*" *Theoria*, 29 (1967), 71−75.

1996 HAYES, T. W., Jr. "The Dialectic of History in Marvell's *Horatian Ode.*" *ClioW*, 1, i (1971), 26−36.

1997 HENSLEY, C. S. "Wither, Waller and Marvell: Panegyrists for the Protector." *ArielE*, 3 (1972), 5−16.

1998 LERNER, L. D. "Andrew Marvell: 'An Horatian Ode upon Cromwell's Return from Ireland.' " *Interpretations: Essays on Twelve English Poems*, ed. J. Wain. London, Boston: Routledge & Kegan Paul, 1955, 1972.

1999 MAZZEO, J. A. "Cromwell as Machiavellian Prince in Marvell's 'An Horatian Ode.' " *JHI*, 21 (1960), 1−17; and see **110.**

2000 MAZZEO, J. A. "Cromwell as Davidic King." See **109** and **110.**

2001 NEVO, R. *The Dial of Virtue.* See **220.**

2002 SELDEN, R. "Historical Thought and Marvell's *Horatian Ode.*" *DUJ*, 34 (1973), 41−53.

2003 STEAD, C. K. "The Actor and the Man of Action: Marvell's 'Horatian Ode.' " *The Critical Survey*, 3 (1967), 145−50.

2004 SYFRET, R. H. "Marvell's 'Horatian Ode.' " *RES*, 12 (1961), 160−72.

2005 WALLACE, J. M. "Marvell's 'Lusty Mate' and the Ship of the Commonwealth." *MLN*, 76 (1961), 106−10.

2006 WALLACE, J. M. "Marvell's 'Horatian Ode.' " *PMLA*, 77 (1962), 33−45.

2007 WALLACE, J. M. "Andrew Marvell and Cromwell's Kingship: 'The First Anniversary.' " *ELH*, 30 (1963), 209−35; and see **1866.**

2008 WILLIAMSON, G. "Bias in Marvell's *Horatian Ode.*" See **139.**

2009 WILSON, A. J. N. "Andrew Marvell: *An Horatian Ode upon Cromwell's Return from Ireland:* The Thread of the Poem and Its Use of Classical Allusion." *CritQ*, 11 (1969), 325−41.

2010 WILSON, A. J. N. "Andrew Marvell's 'The First Anniversary of the Government under Oliver Cromwell': The Poem and its Frame of Reference." *MLR*, 69 (1974), 254−73.

2011 WOOD, W. J. "Marvell's 'An Horatian Ode Upon Cromwell's Return from Ireland.' " *Theoria*, 28 (1967), 57−62.

Henry More (1614—1687)

Editions

2012 *Opera Omnia,* ed. S. Hutin. Hildesheim: Olms, 1966.

2013 *The Complete Poems,* ed. A. B. Grosart. Edinburgh: Constable, 1876, 1878; New York: AMS Press, 1967; Hildesheim: Olms, 1969.

2014 *The Philosophical Poems,* ed. G. Bullough. Manchester: Manchester University Press, 1931.

2015 *Philosophical Writings,* ed. F. I. MacKinnon. New York: Oxford University Press, 1925; New York: AMS Press, 1969.

2016 *Democritus Platonissans (1646),* ed. P. G. Stanwood. Los Angeles: William Andrews Clark Memorial Library, 1968.

2017 *Enchiridion Ethicum . . . , An Account of Virtue,* trans. E. Southwell; 1690. New York: Facsimile Text Society, 1930.

2018 *Enthusiasmus Trimphatus (1662),* ed. M. V. De Porte. Los Angeles: William Andrews Clark Memorial Library, 1967.

2019 *The Conway Letters: The Correspondence of Anne, Vicountess Conway, Henry More, and Their Friends, 1642—1684,* ed. M. H. Nicolson. New Haven: Yale University Press, 1930.

2020 [Selections]: *The Cambridge Platonists,* ed. G. R. Cragg. New York: Oxford University Press, 1968.

2021 [Selections]: The Cambridge Platonists, ed. C. A. Patrides. London: Arnold, 1969.

Bibliography

2022 GUFFEY, G. R., ed. *Traherne and the Seventeenth-Century English Platonists. Elizabethan Bibliographies Supplements,* 11. London: Nether Press, 1969.

Studies

2023 ANDERSON, P. R. *Science in Defense of Religion: A Study of Henry More's Attempt to Link Seventeenth-Century Religion with Science.* New York: Putnam's, 1933.

2024 BAKER, J. T. "Henry More and Kant." *Philosophical Review,* 46 (1937), 298—306.

2025 BROWN, C. C. "The Mere Numbers of Henry More's Cabbala." *SEL,* 10 (1970), 445—54.

HENRY MORE

2026 CASSIRER, E. *The Platonic Renaissance in England.* See **298.**

2027 COLBY, F. L. "Thomas Traherne and Henry More." *MLN,* 62 (1947), 490−92.

2028 COLIE, R. L. *Light and Enlightenement.* . . . See **441.**

2029 DePAULEY, W. C. *The Candle of the Lord: Studies in the Cambridge Platonists.* London: S.P.C.K., 1937.

2030 DOUGHTY, W. L. "A Cynic among Sectaries: Henry More." See **164.**

2031 GREENE, R. A. "Henry More and Robert Boyle on the Spirit of Nature." *JHI,* 23 (1962), 451−74.

2032 HARRISON, A. W. "Henry More, the Cambridge Platonist." *London Quarterly,* 158 (1933), 485−92.

2033 HOYLES, J. *The Waning of the Renaissance, 1640−1740: Studies in the Thought and Poetry of Henry More, John Norris, and Isaac Watts.* The Hague: Nijhoff, 1971.

2034 HUNTER, W. B., Jr. "Plastic Nature . . . ." See **304.**

2035 LICHTENSTEIN, A. *Henry More: The Rational Theology of a Cambridge Platonist.* Cambridge: Harvard University Press, 1962.

2036 MITCHELL, W. F. "The Cambridge Platonists . . . ." See **469.**

2037 NICOLSON, M. H. "More's Psychozoia." *MLN,* 57 (1922), 141−48.

2038 NICOLSON, M. H. "The Spirit World of Milton and More." *SP,* 22 (1925), 433−52.

2039 NICOLSON, M. H. "Milton and the *Conjectura Cabbalistica.*" *PQ,* 6 (1927), 1−18.

2040 NICOLSON, M. H. "The Early Stages of Cartesianism in England." *SP,* 26 (1929), 356−74.

2041 NICOLSON, M. H. *The Breaking of the Circle.* . . . See **221.**

2042 NICOLSON, M. H. *Mountain Gloom and Mountain Glory.* . . . See **117.**

2043 PANICHAS, G. A. "The Greek Spirit and the Mysticism of Henry More." *Greek Orthodox Theological Review,* 2 (1956), 41−61.

2044 PAWSON, G. P. H. "Henry More." *The Cambridge Platonists and their Place in Religious Thought.* London: S.P.C.K., 1930.

2045 POWICKE, F. J. "Henry More." *The Cambridge Platonists.* London: Dent; Cambridge: Harvard University Press, 1926.

2046 RØSTVIG, M.-S. *The Hidden Sense.* New York: Humanities Press, 1963.

2047 TULLOCH, J. *Rational Theology.* . . . See **482.**

2048 WILLEY, B. "Rational Theology: The Cambridge Platonists." See **136.**

Thomas Overbury (1581– 1613)

Editions

2049 *Miscellaneous Works,* ed. E. F. Rimbault. London: Smith, 1856.

2050 *The Overburian Characters, To Which is Added A Wife by Sir Thomas Overbury,* ed. W. J. Paylor. Oxford: Blackwell, 1936.

2051 *The "Conceited News"* . . . , *Sir Thomas Overbury his Wife, 1616,* ed. J. Savage. Gainesville: Scholars Facsimiles & Reprints, 1968.

2052 *Characters: or Witty Descriptions of the Propensities of Sundry Persons.* Chicago: University of Chicago Press, 1967.

2053 *A Book of Characters,* ed. R. Aldington. London: Routledge; New York: Dutton, 1924.

2054 *A Cabinet of Characters,* ed. G. Murphy. London: Oxford University Press, 1925; St. Clair Shores: Scholarly Press, 1972.

2055 *A Mirror of Charactery,* ed. H. Osborne. London: University Tutorial Press, 1933.

Studies

2056 BOYCE, B. "The Overburian Character." See **270.**

2057 BOYCE, B. *The Polemic Character, 1640– 1661.* Lincoln: University of Nebraska Press, 1955.

2058 CLAUSEN, W. "The Beginnings of English Character writing in the Early Seventeenth Century." See **1326.**

2059 THOMPSON, E. N. S. "Character Books." *Literary Bypaths of the Renaissance.* New Haven: Yale University Press, 1924; Freeport: Books for Libraries, 1968.

2060 WHIBLEY, C. "Sir Thomas Overbury." *Essays in Biography.* London: Constable, 1913.

2061 WHITE, B. *Cast of Ravens: The Strange Case of Sir Thomas Overbury.* London: Murray, 1965.

Francis Quarles (1592– 1644)

Editions

2062 *The Complete Works in Prose and Verse,* ed. A. B. Grosart. Edinburgh: Constable, 1880–81; New York: AMS Press, 1967.

2063 *Emblems*, ed. G. Gilfillan. Edinburgh: Nicol, 1857.

2064 *A Selection of Emblems, from Herman Hugo: Pia desiderata; Francis Quarles: Emblemes* . . . , ed. W. A. McQueen. Los Angeles: William Andrews Clark Memorial Library, 1972.

2065 *Hieroglyphikes of the Life of Man*, ed. J. Horden. Menston: Scolar Press, 1969.

2066 *Hosanna . . . and Threnodes*, ed. J. Horden. Liverpool: Liverpool University Press, 1960.

Studies

2067 BEACHCROFT, T. O. "Quarles and the Emblem Habit." *Dublin Review*, 188 (1931), 80 − 96.

2068 DAVIES, H. N. "Quarles's Hybrid Strain." *ELN*, 4 (1967), 266 − 68.

2069 DOUGHTY, W. L. "A Mystic in Half-Lights: Francis Quarles." See **164**.

2070 FREEMAN, R. *English Emblem Books*. See **89**.

2071 HASAN, M. *Francis Quarles: A Study of His Life and Poetry*. Aligarh: Aligarh Muslim University, 1966.

2072 JAMES, E. "The Imagery of Quarles' Emblems." *TSE*, 23 (1943), 26 − 49.

2073 KURTH, B. O. "Old-Testament Heroic Poetry." *Milton and Christian Heroism*. Berkeley: University of California Press, 1959.

2074 NETHERCOT, A. H. "The Literary Legend of Francis Quarles." *MP*, 30 (1923), 225 − 40.

2075 PRAZ, M. *Studies in Seventeenth-Century Imagery*. See **229**.

2076 STEADMAN, J. M. "The Iconographical Background of Quarles' 'Flesh' and 'Spirit.' " *Art Bulletin*, 39 (1957), 231 − 32.

2077 THOMPSON, E. N. S. "Emblem Books." *Literary Bypaths of the Renaissance*. New Haven: Yale University Press, 1924; Freeport: Books for Libraries, 1968.

Henry Reynolds (fl 1628− 1632)

Editions

2078 *Mythomystes*, ed. A. F. Kinney. Menston: Scolar Press, 1972.

2079 *Mythomystes*, ed. E. W. Tayler. See **61**.

2080 *Mythomystes*, ed. J. E. Spingarn. See **59**.

2081 *Torquato Tasso: Aminta*, trans. Henry Reynolds, ed. C. Davidson. Fennimore: Westburg and Associates, 1972.

Studies

2082 CINQUEMANI, A. M. "Henry Reynolds' *Mythomystes* and the Continuity of Ancient Modes of *Allegoresis* in Seventeenth-Century England." *PMLA*, 85 (1970), 1041−49.

2083 SEWELL, E. *The Orphic Voice.* See **236.**

John Suckling (1609− 1642)

Editions

2084 *The Works,* ed. T. Clayton and L. A. Beaurline. Oxford: Clarendon Press, 1971.

2085 *The Works in Prose and Verse,* ed. A. H. Thompson. London: Routledge; New York: Dutton, 1910; New York: Russell & Russell, 1964.

2086 *Poems and Letters from Manuscript,* ed. H. Berry. London, Ont.: University of Western Ontario, 1960.

2087 *Minor Poets of the Seventeenth Century,* ed. R. G. Howarth. New York: Dutton, 1931.

2088 [Selections], ed. H. N. Maclean. See **47.**

Studies

2089 ANSELMENT, R. A. " 'Men Most of All Enjoy, When Least They Do': The Love Poetry of John Suckling." *TSLL*, 14 (1972), 17−32.

2090 BALD, R. C. "A Note on Suckling's 'A Session of the Poets.' " *MLN*, 58 (1943), 550−51.

2091 BEAURLINE, L. A. "The Canon of Sir John Suckling's Poems." *SP*, 57 (1960), 105−26.

2092 BEAURLINE, L. A. "New Poems by Sir John Suckling." *SP*, 59 (1962), 651−57.

2093 BEAURLINE, L. A. " 'Why So Pale and Wan': An Essay in Critical Method." *TSLL*, 4 (1962), 553−63.

2094 BEAURLINE, L. A. "An Editorial Experiment: Suckling's *A Session of the Poets.*" *SB*, 16 (1963), 43−60.

2095 BENHAM, A. R. "Suckling's 'A Session of the Poets.' " *MLQ*, 6 (1945), 21−27.

2096 CANDELANS, F. H. "Ovid and the Indifferent Lovers." *RN*, 13 (1960), 294−97.

2097 GRAY, P. H. "Suckling's 'A Session of the Poets' as a Ballad." *SP*, 36 (1939), 60−69.

2098 HENDERSON, F. O. "Traditions of *Précieux* and *Libertin* in Suckling's Poetry." *ELH*, 4 (1937), 274−98.

2099 MINER, E. *The Cavalier Mode.* See **216.**

2100 SUMMERS, J. H. "Gentlemen of the Court and of Art: Suckling. . . . " See **246.**

2101 WALLERSTEIN, R. C. "Suckling's Imitation of Shakespeare: A Caroline View of His Art." *RES*, 19 (1943), 290−95.

Jeremy Taylor (1613− 1667)

Editions

2102 *Works,* ed. R. Heber and C. P. Eden. London: Longmans, Brown, 1847−54.

2103 *Jeremy Taylor: A Selection,* ed. M. Armstrong. Waltham St. Lawrence: Golden Cockerel Press, 1923.

2104 *The Golden Grove: Selected Passages from the Sermons and Writings,* ed. L. P. Smith. Oxford: Clarendon Press, 1930.

2105 *The Rule and Exercise of Holy Living,* ed. T. S. Kepler. Cleveland: World Publishing, 1952.

2106 *Holy Living and Holy Dying,* ed. A. R. Waller. London: Longmans, Green, 1900, 1923.

2107 *The House of Understanding: Selections,* ed. M. Gest. Philadelphia: University of Pennsylvania Press, 1954.

2108 *Poems and Verse-Translations,* ed. A. B. Grosart. Edinburgh: Blackburn: 1870.

Bibliography

2109 GATHORNE-HARDY, R., and W. P. WILLIAMS. *A Bibliography of the Writings of Jeremy Taylor to 1700.* DeKalb: Northern Illinois University Press, 1971.

Studies

2110 ADDISON, J. T. "Jeremy Taylor, Preacher and Pastor." *Historical Magazine of the Protestant Episcopal Church,* 21 (1949), 148−90.

2111 ANTOINE, Sr. M. S. *The Rhetoric of Jeremy Taylor's Prose: Ornament of the Sunday Sermons.* Washington, D.C.: Catholic University of America, 1946.

2112 BENTLEY, G. B. "Jeremy Taylor's *Ductor Dubitantium.*" *Theology,* 1 (1947), 182–86.

2113 BOLTON, F. R. *The Caroline Tradition of the Church of Ireland, With Particular Reference to Bishop Jeremy Taylor.* London: S.P.C.K., 1958.

2114 BRINKLEY, R. F. "Coleridge's Criticism of Jeremy Taylor." *HLQ,* 13 (1949–50), 313–23.

2115 BROWN, W. J. *Jeremy Taylor.* New York: Macmillan, 1925.

2116 BRUSH, J. "*The Liberty of Prophesying:* A Tercentenary Essay." *Crozier Quarterly,* 25 (1948), 116–23.

2117 COX, G. H., III. "A Re-evaluation of Jeremy Taylor's *Holy Living* and *Holy Dying.*" *NM,* 73 (1972), 836–48.

2118 ELMEN, P. "Jeremy Taylor and the Fall of Man." *MLQ,* 14 (1953), 139–48.

2119 GLICKSMAN, H. "The Figurative Quality in Jeremy Taylor's *Holy Dying.*" *SR,* 30 (1922), 488–94.

2120 HERNDON, S. *The Use of the Bible in Jeremy Taylor's Works.* New York: New York University Press, 1949.

2121 HOOPES, R. G. "Voluntarism in Jeremy Taylor and the Platonic Tradition." *HLQ,* 13 (1949–50), 341–54.

2122 HUGHES, H. T. *The Piety of Jeremy Taylor.* New York: St. Martin's, 1960.

2123 HUNTLEY, F. L. *Jeremy Taylor and the Great Rebellion: A Study of His Mind and Temper in Controversy.* Ann Arbor: University of Michigan Press, 1970.

2124 KING, J. R. "Certain Aspects of Jeremy Taylor's Prose Style." *ES,* 37 (1956), 197–210.

2125 KING, J. R. *Studies in Seventeenth-Century Writers.* See **103.**

2126 McADOO, H. R. *The Structure of Caroline Moral Theology.* See **463** and **464.**

2127 MITCHELL, W. F. "Jeremy Taylor." See **469.**

2128 NICOLSON, M. H. "New Material on Jeremy Taylor." *PQ,* 8 (1929), 321–34.

2129 NOSSEN, R. "Jeremy Taylor: Seventeenth-Century Theologian." *ATR,* 42 (1960), 28–39.

2130 STEFFAN, T. G. "Jeremy Taylor's Criticism of Abstract Speculation." *TSE,* 20 (1940), 96–108.

2131 STRANKS, C. J. *The Life and Writings of Jeremy Taylor.* London: S.P.C.K., 1952.

2132 STRANKS, C. J. "Holy Living and Holy Dying." See **480.**

2133 TULLOCH, J. *Rational Theology and Christian Philosophy.* See **482.**

2134 WILEY, M. L. "Jeremy Taylor, the Sceptic as Churchman." *WHR,* 4 (1950), 3–17; and see **134.**

2135 WILLIAMSON, H. R. *Jeremy Taylor.* London: Pegasus, 1952.

2136 WOOD, T. *English Casuistical Divinity during the Seventeenth Century: With Special Reference to Jeremy Taylor.* London: S.P.C.K., 1952.

Thomas Traherne (1637—1674)

Editions

2137 *Centuries, Poems, and Thanksgivings,* ed. H. M. Margoliouth. Oxford: Clarendon Press, 1958.

2138 *Poems, Centuries, and Three Thanksgivings,* ed. A. Ridler. New York: Oxford University Press, 1966.

2139 *Poems of Felicity,* ed. H. I. Bell. Oxford: Clarendon Press, 1910.

2140 *The Poetical Works,* ed. G. I. Wade. London: Dobell, 1932; New York: Cooper Square, 1965.

2141 *Centuries of Meditations,* ed. B. Dobell. London: Dobell, 1908, etc.; introd. J. Hayward, 1950; introd. H. Vaughan, 1960.

2142 *Centuries,* ed. J. Farrar. New York: Harper, 1960.

2143 *The Way to Blessedness: . . . Christian Ethicks,* ed. M. Bottrall. London: Faith Press, 1962.

2144 *Christian Ethicks,* ed. C. L. Marks and G. R. Guffey. Ithaca: Cornell University Press, 1968.

2145 *Meditations on the Six Days of the Creation,* ed. G. R. Guffey. Los Angeles: Clark Memorial Library, University of Los Angeles, 1966.

2146 *A Serious and Pathetical Contemplation of the Mercies of God, in . . . Thanksgivings . . . ,* ed. R. Daniells. Toronto: University of Toronto Press, 1941.

Bibliographies and Concordance

2147 BERRY, L. E., ed. "Thomas Traherne: [Bibliography]." See **4.**

2148 CLEMENTS, A. L., ed. "Thomas Traherne: A Chronological Bibliography." *Library Chronicle,* 35 (1969), 36—51.

2149 DEES, J. S., ed. "Recent Studies in Traherne." *ELR,* 4 (1974), 189—96.

2150 GUFFEY, G. R., ed. *Traherne and the Seventeenth-Century English Platonists. Elizabethan Bibliographies Supplements,* 11. London: Nether Press, 1969.

2151 GUFFEY, G. R., ed. *A Concordance to the Poetry of Thomas Traherne.* Berkeley: University of California Press, 1974.

2152 SPENCER, T., ed. "Thomas Traherne: [Bibliography]." See **17.**

Studies

2153 BEACHCROFT, T. O. "Traherne and the Cambridge Platonists." *Dublin Review,* 186 (1930), 278—90.

2154 BOTTRALL, M. "Thomas Traherne's Praise of Creation." *CritQ,* 1 (1959), 126−33.

2155 BROWN, R. M. "Knowledge and the Fall of Man: Traherne's *Centuries* and Milton's *Paradise Lost." LURev,* 4 (1971), 41−49.

2156 CLEMENTS, A. L. "On the Mode and Meaning of Traherne's Mystical Poetry: 'The Preparative.' " *SP,* 61 (1964), 500−521.

2157 CLEMENTS, A. L. *The Mystical Poetry of Thomas Traherne.* Cambridge: Harvard University Press, 1969.

2158 COLBY, F. L. "Thomas Traherne and Henry More." *MLN,* 62 (1947), 490−92.

2159 COLIE, R. L. "Thomas Traherne and the Infinite: The Ethical Compromise." *HLQ,* 21 (1957), 69−82.

2160 COX, G. H., III. "Traherne's *Centuries*: A Platonic Devotion of 'Divine Philosophy.' " *MP,* 69 (1971), 10−24.

2161 DAY, M. M. "Traherne and the Doctrine of Pre-existence." *SP,* 65 (1968), 81−97.

2162 DAY, M. M. " 'Naked Truth' and the Language of Thomas Traherne." *SP,* 68 (1971), 305−25.

2163 DOUGHTY, W. L. "Songs of Spiritual 'Felicitie.' " See **164.**

2164 DRAKE, B. "Thomas Traherne's Songs of Innocence." *MP,* 31 (1970), 492−503.

2165 ELLRODT, R. *L'inspiration personelle . . . chez les poetes metaphysique anglais.* See **169.**

2166 GILBERT, A. H. "Thomas Traherne as Artist." *MLQ,* 8 (1947), 319−41, 435−47.

2167 GOLDKNOPF, D. "The Disintegration of Symbol in a Meditative Poet." *CE,* 30 (1968), 48−59.

2168 GRANT, P. "Original Sin and the Fall of Man in Thomas Traherne." *ELH,* 38 (1971), 40−61.

2169 GRANT, P. "Irenaean Theodicy and Thomas Traherne." See **178.**

2170 GUFFEY, G. R. "Thomas Traherne on Original Sin." *N&Q,* 14 (1967), 98−100.

2171 HANLEY, Sr. K. "Thomas Traherne's *Centuries of Meditation:* Structure and Style." *CSR,* 3 (1973), 38−43.

2172 HEPBURN, R. W. "Thomas Traherne: The Nature and Dignity of Imagination." *Cambridge Journal,* 6 (1952−53), 725−34.

2173 IREDALE, Q. *Thomas Traherne.* Oxford: Blackwell, 1935.

2174 JENNINGS, E. " 'The Accessible Art': A Study of Thomas Traherne's *Centuries of Meditations." TC,* 167 (1960), 140−51; and *Every Changing Shape*; Philadelphia: Dufour, 1961.

2175 JORDAN, R. D. *The Temple of Eternity: Thomas Traherne's Philosophy of Time.* Port Washington: Kennikat, 1972.

2176 KING, A. "Thomas Traherne: Intellect and Felicity." *Restoration Literature: Critical Approaches,* ed. H. Love. London: Methuen; New York: Barnes and Noble, 1972.

2177 LEISHMAN, J. B. "Thomas Traherne." See **201.**

2178 MARKS, C. L. "Thomas Traherne and Cambridge Platonism." *PMLA,* 81 (1966), 521—34.

2179 MARKS, C. L. "Thomas Traherne and Hermes Trismegistus." *RN,* 19 (1966), 118—31.

2180 MARKS, C. L. "Traherne's Church's Year-Book." *PBSA,* 60 (1966), 31—72.

2181 MARKS, C. L. "Thomas Traherne's Early Studies." *PBSA,* 62 (1968), 511—36.

2182 MARSHALL, W. H. "Thomas Traherne and the Doctrine of Original Sin." *MLN,* 73 (1958), 161—65.

2183 MARTZ, L. L. "Thomas Traherne: Confessions of Paradise." See **208.**

2184 McFARLAND, R. E. "Thomas Traherne's *Thanksgivings* and the Theology of Optimism." *EnlE,* 4 (1973), 3—14.

2185 McFARLAND, R. E. "From Ambiguity to Paradox: Thomas Traherne's 'Things.' " *Wascana Review,* 9 (1974), 114—23.

2186 MIMS, E. "Thomas Traherne: Poet of Felicity." *The Christ of the Poets.* Nashville: Abingdon, 1948.

2187 MINER, E. *The Metaphysical Mode.* See **215.**

2188 RIDLON, H. G. "The Function of the 'Infant-Ey' in Traherne's Poetry." *SP,* 61 (1964), 627—39.

2189 RØSTVIG, M.-S. *The Happy Man.* See **320.**

2190 RUSSELL, A. "The Life of Thomas Traherne." *RES,* 6 (1955), 34—43.

2191 SALTER, K. W. *Thomas Traherne: Mystic and Poet.* London: Arnold, 1964; New York: Barnes & Noble, 1965.

2192 SANDBANK, S. "Thomas Traherne on the Place of Man in the Universe." *Scripta Hierosolymitana: Studies in English Language and Literature,* 17 (1966), 121—36.

2193 SAULS, L. "Traherne's Debt to Puente's Meditations." *PQ,* 50 (1971), 161—74.

2194 SHERRINGTON, A. J. *Mystical Symbolism in the Poetry of Thomas Traherne.* St. Lucia: University of Queensland, 1970.

2195 STALEY, T. F. "The Theocentric Vision of Thomas Traherne." *Cithara,* 4 (1964), 43—47.

2196 STEWART, S. *The Expanded Voice: The Art of Thomas Traherne.* San Marino: Huntington Library, 1970.

2197 STRANKS, C. J. "Centuries of Meditation." See **480.**

2198 TRIMPY, J. E. "An Analysis of Traherne's 'Thoughts I.' " *SP,* 68 (1971), 88—104.

2199 UPHAUS, R. "Thomas Traherne: Perception as Process." *UWR,* 3, ii (1968), 19—27.

2200 WADE, G. I. *Thomas Traherne: A Critical Biography.* London: Oxford University Press; Princeton: Princeton University Press, 1944.

2201 WAHL, J. "Thomas Traherne." *EA,* 14 (1961), 117—23.

2202 WALLACE, J. M. "Thomas Traherne and the Structure of Meditation." *ELH,* 25 (1958), 79—89.

2203 WEBBER, J. " 'I and Thou' in the Prose of Thomas Traherne." *PLL*, 2 (1966), 258–64.

2204 WEBBER, J. "Thomas Traherne: The Fountain of Love." See **287**.

2205 WHITE, H. C. "Thomas Traherne. . . . " See **262**.

2206 WILLIAMS, M. G. "Thomas Traherne: Center of God's Wealth." *Cithara*, 3 (1963), 32–40.

2207 WILLY, M. "Thomas Traherne: Felicity's Perfect Lover." *English*, 12 (1959), 210–15.

2208 WILLY, M. "Thomas Traherne." See **266**.

2209 WOODHOUSE, A. S. P. *The Poet and His Faith*. Chicago: University of Chicago Press, 1965.

Henry Vaughan (1622– 1695)

Editions

2210 *The Works in Verse and Prose*, ed. A. B. Grosart. Edinburgh: Blackburn, 1871; New York: AMS Press, 1970.

2211 *The Works*, ed. L. C. Martin. Oxford: Clarendon Press, 1914; second edition, 1957.

2212 *The Works*, ed. A. E. Waite. New Hyde Park: University Books, 1969.

2213 *Poetry and Selected Prose*, ed. L. C. Martin. London: Oxford University Press, 1963.

2214 *The Complete Poetry*, ed. F. Fogle. Garden City: Doubleday, 1964; New York: Norton, 1969.

2215 *The Secular Poems*, ed. E. L. Marilla. Cambridge: Harvard University Press, 1958.

2216 *A Selection*, ed. C. Dixon. London: Longmans, 1967.

Bibliographies and Concordance

2217 BERRY, L. E., ed. "Henry Vaughan: [Bibliography]." See **14**.

2218 BOURDETTE, R. E., Jr., ed. "Recent Studies in Henry Vaughan." *ELR*, 4 (1974), 299–310.

2219 MARILLA, E. L., ed. *A Comprehensive Bibliography of Henry Vaughan*. Tuscaloosa: University of Alabama Press, 1948.

2220 MARILLA, E. L., and J. D. SIMMONDS, eds. *Henry Vaughan: A Bibliographical Supplement, 1946– 1960*. Tuscaloosa: University of Alabama Press, 1963.

2221 SPENCER, T., ed. "Henry Vaughan: [Bibliography]." See **17**.

2222 TUTTLE, I., ed. *Concordance to Vaughan's "Silex Scintillans."* University Park: Pennsylvania State University Press, 1969.

Studies

2223 ALLEN, D. C. "Henry Vaughan: 'Cock-Crowing.' " See **142**.

2224 BARKSDALE, R. K. "The Nature Poetry of Henry Vaughan." *WHR,* 9 (1955), 341–48.

2225 BENNETT, J. "Henry Vaughan." See **148**.

2226 BETHELL, S. L. "The Theology of Henry and Thomas Vaughan." *Theology,* 56 (1953), 137–43.

2227 BETHELL, S. L. "The Poetry of Henry Vaughan, Silurist." See **76**.

2228 BLUNDEN, E. C. *On the Poems of Henry Vaughan: Characteristics and Intimations, with his Principal Latin Poems Carefully Translated into English Verse.* London: Cobden-Sanderson, 1927.

2229 BOWERS, F. "The Star Symbol in Henry Vaughan's Poetry." *RenP* (1962), 25–29.

2230 BOWERS, F. "Henry Vaughan's Multiple Time Scheme." *MLQ,* 23 (1962), 291–96.

2231 BROOKS, C. "Henry Vaughan: Quietism and Mysticism." *Essays in Honor of E. L. Marilla,* ed. T. A. Kirby and W. J. Olive. Baton Rouge: Louisiana State University Press, 1970.

2232 CHAMBERS, L. H. "Henry Vaughan's Allusive Technique: Biblical Allusion in 'The NIght.' " *MLQ,* 27 (1966), 137–50.

2233 CHAMBERS, L. H. "Vaughan's 'The World': The Limits of Extrinsic Criticism." *SEL,* 8 (1968), 137–50.

2234 CHAPMAN, A. V. "Henry Vaughan and Magnetic Philosophy." *SoRA,* 4 (1971), 215–26.

2235 CHRISTOPHER, G. B. "In Arcadia, Calvin . . . : A Study of Nature in Henry Vaughan." *SP,* 70 (1973), 408–26.

2236 CLOUGH, W. O. "Henry Vaughan and the Hermetic Philosophy." *PMLA,* 48 (1933), 1108–30.

2237 DALE, J. "Biblical Allusion in Vaughan's 'The World.' " *ES,* 51 (1970), 336–39.

2238 DOUGHTY, W. L. "Religion under the Stars." See **164**.

2239 DURR, R. A. "Vaughan's Theme and its Pattern: 'Regeneration.' " *SP,* 54 (1957), 14–28.

2240 DURR, R. A. "Vaughan's 'The Night.' " *JEGP,* 59 (1960), 34–40.

2241 DURR, R. A. "Vaughan's Pilgrim and the Birds of Night: 'The Proffer.' " *MLQ,* 21 (1960), 45–58.

2242 DURR, R. A. "Vaughan's Spring on a Hill." *MLN,* 76 (1961), 704–7.

2243 DURR, R. A. *On the Mystical Poetry of Henry Vaughan.* Cambridge: Harvard University Press, 1962.

2244 DUVALL, R. "The Biblical Character of Henry Vaughan's *Silex Scintillans.*" *PCP,* 6 (1971), 13—19.

2245 ELLRODT, R. *L'inspiration personelle . . . chez les poètes metaphysique anglais.* See **169.**

2246 FARNHAM, F. "The Imagery of Vaughan's 'The Night.' " *PQ,* 38 (1959), 425—35.

2247 FRANCIS, W. N. "Vaughan's *The Waterfall.*" *Expl,* 14 (1956), Item 57.

2248 GARNER, R. *Henry Vaughan: Experience and the Tradition.* Chicago: University of Chicago Press, 1959.

2249 GARNER, R. *The Unprofitable Servant in Henry Vaughan.* Lincoln: University of Nebraska Press, 1963.

2250 GRANT, P. "Hermetic Philosophy and the Nature of Man in Vaughan's *Silex Scintillans. JEGP,* 67 (1968), 406—22.

2251 GRANT, P. "Henry Vaughan and the Hermetic Philosophy." See **178.**

2252 HALEWOOD, W. H. " . . . Vaughan: The Psalm Model of Reconciliation." See **180.**

2253 HILBERRY, C. "Vaughan's 'The Morning-Watch.' " *Expl,* 14 (1956), Item 44.

2254 HOLMES, E. *Henry Vaughan and the Hermetic Philosophy.* Oxford: Blackwell, 1932; New York: Russell & Russell, 1967.

2255 HUGHES, M. Y. "The Theme of Pre-Existence and Infancy in 'The Retreate.' " *PQ,* 20 (1941), 484—500.

2256 HUTCHINSON, F. E. *Henry Vaughan: A Life and Interpretation.* Oxford: Clarendon Press, 1947.

2257 KERMODE, F. "The Private Imagery of Henry Vaughan." *RES,* 1 (1950), 206—25.

2258 KING, J. R. "Pilgrimage to Paradise: Center of Vaughan's Religious World." See **103.**

2259 KREGOR, K. H. "Henry Vaughan and Natural Magic." *ForumH,* 9, i (1971), 82—86.

2260 LEE, K. S. "The Poetry of Henry Vaughan." *English Language and Literature* (Korea), 11 (1962), 28—50.

2261 LEHMAN, R. P. "Henry Vaughan and Welsh Poetry." *PQ,* 24 (1945), 329—42.

2262 LEISHMAN, J. B. "Henry Vaughan." See **201.**

2263 LESSENICH, R. P. "Henry Vaughan's Poem 'Regeneration.' " *SN,* 44 (1972), 76—89.

2264 MAHOOD, M. M. "Vaughan: The Symphony of Nature." See **204.**

2265 MARILLA, E. L. "The Significance of Henry Vaughan's Literary Reputation." *MLQ,* 5 (1944), 155—62.

2266 MARILLA, E. L. "Henry and Thomas Vaughan." *MLR,* 39 (1944), 180—83.

2267 MARILLA, E. L. "The Religious Conversion of Henry Vaughan." *RES,* 21 (1945), 15—22.

2268 MARILLA, E. L. "Henry Vaughan's Conversion: A Recent View." *MLN*, 63 (1948), 394—97.

2269 MARILLA, E. L. "The Secular and Religious Poetry of Henry Vaughan." *MLQ*, 9 (1948), 394—411.

2270 MARILLA, E. L. "The Mysticism of Henry Vaughan: Some Observations." *RES*, 18 (1967), 164—66.

2271 MARTIN, L. C. "Henry Vaughan and the Theme of Infancy." See **123**.

2272 MARTZ, L. L. "Henry Vaughan: The Man Within." *PMLA*, 78 (1963), 40—49.

2273 MARTZ, L. L. *The Poetry of Meditation.* See **206**.

2274 MARTZ, L. L. "Henry Vaughan: The Caves of Memory." See **208**.

2275 MINER, E. *The Metaphysical Mode.* See **215**.

2276 MINER, E. *The Cavalier Mode.* See **216**.

2277 MURRIN, M. *The Veil of Allegory: Some Notes Toward a Theory of Allegorical Rhetoric in the English Renaissance.* Chicago: University of Chicago Press, 1969.

2278 OLIVER, H. J. "The Mysticism of Henry Vaughan: A Reply." *JEGP*, 53 (1954), 352—60.

2279 OLSON, P. A. "Vaughan's 'The World': The Pattern of Meaning and the Tradition." *CL*, 13 (1961), 26—32.

2280 PETTET, E. C. *Of Paradise and Light: A Study of Vaughan's "Silex Scintillans."* Cambridge: Cambridge University Press, 1960.

2281 RICKEY, M. E. "Vaughan, *The Temple,* and Poetic Form." *SP*, 59 (1962), 162—70.

2282 RØSTVIG, M.-S. "Syncretic Imagery and the Unity of Vaughan's 'The World.' " *PLL*, 5 (1969), 415—22.

2283 RØSTVIG, M.-S. *The Happy Man.* See **320**.

2284 RUDRUM, A. W. "Henry Vaughan's 'The Book.' " *AUMLA*, 16 (1961), 161—66.

2285 RUDRUM, A. W. "Henry Vaughan and the Theme of Transfiguration." *SoRA*, 1 (1963), 54—68.

2286 RUDRUM, A. W. "Vaughan's 'The Night': Some Hermetic Notes." *MLR*, 64 (1969), 11—19.

2287 RUDRUM, A. "The Influence of Alchemy in the Poems of Henry Vaughan." *PQ*, 49 (1970), 469—80.

2288 RUDRUM, A. "An Aspect of Vaughan's Hermeticism: The Doctrine of Sympathy." *SEL*, 14 (1974), 130—38.

2289 SANDBANK, S. "Henry Vaughan's Apology for Darkness." *SEL*, 7 (1967), 141—52.

2290 SANDLER, F. "The Ascents of the Spirit: Henry Vaughan on the Atonement." *JEGP*, 73 (1974), 209—26.

2291 SIMMONDS, J. D. "The Problem of Henry Vaughan's Illness." *Anglia*, 78 (1960), 353—56.

2292 SIMMONDS, J. D. "Henry Vaughan and the Great Chain of Being." *Studies in English Renaissance Literature,* ed. W. F. McNeir. Baton Rouge: Louisiana State University Press, 1962.

2293 SIMMONDS, J. D. "Some Traditional Oxymora in Vaughan's Secular Verse." *NS,* 11 (1962), 569—73.

2294 SIMMONDS, J. D. "Vaughan's Masterpiece and Its Critics: 'The World' Revaluated." *SEL,* 2 (1962), 77—94.

2295 SIMMONDS, J. D. "Vaughan's 'The Book': Hermetic or Meditative?" *Neophil,* 47 (1963), 320—28.

2296 SIMMONDS, J. D. "Vaughan's Love Poetry." *Essays in Honor of E. L. Marilla,* ed. T. A. Kirby and W. J. Olive. Baton Rouge: Louisiana State University Press, 1970.

2297 SIMMONDS, J. D. *Masques of God: Form and Theme in the Poetry of Henry Vaughan.* Pittsburg: University of Pittsburg Press, 1972.

2298 SMITH, A. J. "Henry Vaughan's Ceremony of Innocence." *E&S,* 26 (1973), 35—52.

2299 SPITZ, L. "Process and Stasis: Aspects of Nature in Vaughan and Marvell." *HLQ,* 32 (1968—69), 135—47.

2300 STEPHENS, J. "Hermetic Symbols and the Christian Context in Vaughan's Poetry." *EN,* 3 (1968—69), 21—24.

2301 STEWART, B. T. "Hermetic Symbolism in Henry Vaughan's 'The Night.' " *PQ,* 29 (1950), 417—22.

2302 STEWART, S. *The Enclosed Garden.* See **245.**

2303 SUMMERS, J. H. *The Heirs of Donne and Jonson.* See **246.**

2304 UNDERWOOD, H. H. "Time and Space in the Poetry of Vaughan." *SP,* 69 (1972), 231—41.

2305 WALTERS, R. H. "Henry Vaughan and the Alchemists." *RES,* 23 (1947), 107—22.

2306 WANAMAKER, M. C. "The Metaphysical Wit of Henry Vaughan's *Silex Scintillans.*" *TSLL,* 16 (1974), 463—78.

2307 WHITE, H. C. "Henry Vaughan. . . . " See **262.**

2308 WIEHE, R. E. "Two Images in Vaughan." *ES,* 45 (1964), 457—60.

2309 WILLIAMSON, G. "Structure in Vaughan's Poetry." See **139.**

2310 WILLY, M. "Henry Vaughan." See **266.**

2311 WILSON, G. E. "A Characteristic of Vaughan's Style and Two Meditative Poems: 'Corruption' and 'Day of Judgement.' " *Style,* 4 (1970), 119—31.

2312 WOODHOUSE, A. S. P. *The Poet and His Faith.* Chicago: University of Chicago Press, 1965.

Edmund Waller (1606– 1687)

Editions

2313 *The Poems,* ed. G. Thorn-Drury. London: Routledge; New York: Scribner's, 1893, 1904.

2314 [*Selections*], ed. H. N. Maclean. See **47**.

Studies

2315 ALLISON, A. W. *Toward an Augustan Poetic: Edmund Waller's "Reform" of English Poetry.* Lexington: University of Kentucky Press, 1962.

2316 BATESON, F. W. "A Word for Waller." *English Poetry: A Critical Introduction.* New York: Barnes & Noble, 1966.

2317 CHERNAIK, W. L. "Waller's Panegyric to My Lord Protector and the Poetry of Praise." *SEL,* 4 (1964), 109–24.

2318 CHERNAIK, W. L. *The Poetry of Limitation: A Study of Edmund Waller.* New Haven: Yale University Press, 1968.

2319 HENSLEY, C. S. "Wither, Waller and Marvell: Panegyrists for the Protector." *ArielE,* 3 (1972), 5–16.

2320 HÖLTGEN, K. J. "Why Was Man Created in the Evening? On Waller's 'An Apologie for Having Loved Before.' " *MLR,* 69 (1974), 23–28.

2321 JOHNSON, S. "Edmund Waller." See **47** and **193**.

2322 KORSHIN, P. J. "The Evolution of Neoclassic Poetics. . . . " See **198**.

2323 LARSON, C. "The Somerset House Poems of Cowley and Waller." *PLL,* 10 (1974), 126–35.

2324 MINER, E. *The Cavalier Mode.* See **216**.

2325 NEVO, R. *The Dial of Virtue.* See **220**.

2326 RICHMOND, H. M. "The Intangible Mistress." *MP,* 56 (1959), 217–23.

2327 RICHMOND, H. M. "The Fate of Edmund Waller." *SAQ,* 60 (1961), 230–38; and see **47**.

2328 RICHMOND, H. M. *The School of Love.* See **231**.

2329 SHARP, R. L. *From Donne to Dryden.* See **238**.

2330 WALLERSTEIN, R. C. "The Development of the Rhetoric and Metre of the Heroic Couplet." See **253**.

2331 WILLIAMSON, G. "The Rhetorical Pattern of Neo-Classical Wit." See **138**.

Izaak Walton (1593– 1683)

Editions

2332 *The Compleat Angler; The Lives . . .* , ed. G. Keynes. London: Nonesuch, 1929.

2333 *The Complete Angler.* London: Nelson, 1925, etc.

2334 *The Compleat Angler,* Nieuwkoop: Miland, 1970.

2335 *The Compleat Angler,* ed. M. Bottrall. London: Dent: New York: Dutton, 1964.

2336 *The Compleat Angler,* ed. J. Buchan. London: Oxford University Press, 1935, 1960.

2337 *The Compleat Angler,* ed. G. Hermes. Baltimore: Penguin, 1939.

2338 *The Complete Angler,* ed. A. Lang. London: Dent, 1958.

2339 *The Compleat Angler,* ed. J. Thompson. New York: Collier, 1962.

2340 *The Lives.* London: Nelson, 1932, 1962.

2341 *The Lives,* ed. S. B. Carter. London: Falcon, 1951.

2342 *The Lives,* ed. G. Saintsbury. London: Oxford University Press, 1927, etc.

2343 *The Lives of Donne and Herbert,* ed. S. C. Roberts. Cambridge: Cambridge University Press, 1957.

Bibliography

2344 DONOVAN, D., ed. "Recent Studies in . . . Walton." *ELR,* 1 (1971), 294 – 303.

Studies

2345 BALD, R. C. "Historical Doubts Respecting Walton's *Life of Donne.*" *Essays in English Literature from the Renaissance to the Victorian Age,* ed. M. MacLure and F. W. Watt. Toronto: University of Toronto Press, 1964.

2346 BENNETT, R. E. "Walton's Use of Donne's Letters." *PQ,* 16 (1937), 30 – 34.

2347 BENNETT, H. R. "Izaak Walton: The Compleat Layman." *ATR,* 46 (1965), 83 – 88.

2348 BOTTRALL, M. *Izaak Walton.* London: Longmans, Green, 1955.

2349 BUTT, J. "Izaak Walton's Methods of Biography." *E&S,* 19 (1933), 67 – 84.

2350 BUTT, J. *Biography in the Hands of Walton, Johnson, Boswell.* Los Angeles: University of California Press, 1966.

2351 COOPER, J. R. "The Art of *The Compleat Angler.*" Durham: Duke University Press, 1968.

2352 GOLDMAN, M. S. "Izaak Walton and *The Arte of Angling,* 1577." See **68.**

2353 GREENSLADE, B. D. "*The Compleat Angler* and the Sequestered Clergy." *RES,* 5 (1954), 361–66.

2354 HELTZEL, V. B. "Isaak Walton's Motto." *HLQ,* 18 (1955), 415–19.

2355 KRUEGER, R. "The Publication of John Donne's Sermons." *RES,* 15 (1964), 151–60.

2356 MANLEY, F. "Walton's *Angler* and Donne: A Probable Allusion." *MLN,* 76 (1961), 13–15.

2357 MARTIN, S. *Izaak Walton and His Friends.* London: Chapman & Hall, 1903; revised edition, 1904.

2358 MOLDENHAWER, J. V. "The Faith of Izaak Walton." *Religion in Life,* 16 (1947), 336–43.

2359 NOVARR, D. *The Making of Walton's Lives.* Ithaca: Cornell University Press, 1958.

2360 OLIVER, A. "Izaak Walton and the Classics." *Classical Weekly,* 38 (May 14, 1945), 179–80.

2361 OLIVER, H. J. "Isaak Walton's Prose Style." *RES,* 21 (1945), 280–88.

2362 OLIVER, H. J. "The Composition and Revisions of *The Compleat Angler.*" *MLR,* 42 (1947), 296–313.

2363 OLIVER, P. *A New Chronicle of "The Complete Angler."* London: Williams & Norgate, 1936.

2364 PAMP, F. E., Jr. "Walton's Redaction of Hooker." *CH,* 17 (1948), 95–116.

2365 SILVER, L. "The First Edition of Walton's *Life of Herbert.*" *HLB,* 5 (1951), 371–72.

2366 STAUFFER, D. "Izaak Walton." See **285.**

George Wither (1588– 1667)

Editions

2367 *The Poetry,* ed. F. Sidgwick. London: Bullen, 1902; New York: AMS Press, 1968.

2368 *A Collection of Emblemes, Ancient and Moderne* (1635), introd. by R. Freeman; notes by C. S. Hensley. *Renaissance Text Society Publications,* V–VI. Columbia: University of South Carolina Press for The Newberry Library, 1975.

2369 *History of the Pestilence,* ed. J. M. French. Cambridge: Harvard University Press, 1930.

Studies

2370 CALHOUN, T. O. "George Wither: Origins and Consequences of a Loose Poetics." *TSLL*, 16 (1974), 263—92.

2371 DALY, P. M. "The Semantics of the Emblem: Recent Developments in Emblem Theory." *Wascana Review*, 9 (1974), 199—212.

2372 GRUNDY, J. "The Early Poetry of George Wither." See **179**.

2373 HENSLEY, C. S. *The Later Career of George Wither*. The Hague: Mouton, 1969.

2374 HENSLEY, C. S. "Wither, Waller and Marvell: Panegyrists for the Protector." *ArielE*, 3 (1972), 5—16.

2375 PRITCHARD, A. "Wither's Motto and Browne's *Religio Medici*." *PQ*, 40 (1961), 302—7.

2376 PRITCHARD, A. "George Wither: The Poet as Prophet." *SP*, 59 (1962), 211—30.

2377 PRITCHARD, A. "*Abuses Stript and Whipt* and Wither's Imprisonment." *RES*, 14 (1963), 337—45.

Henry Wotton (1568— 1639)

Editions

2378 *The Poems of Sir Walter Raleigh . . . , with Those of Sir Henry Wotton . . . ,* ed. J. Hannah. London: Bell, 1892.

2379 *The Elements of Architecture. Complaint and Reform in England, 1436— 1714,* ed. W. H. Dunham and S. Pargellis. New York: Oxford University Press, 1938; New York: Octagon, 1968.

2380 *A Philosophical Survey of Education or Moral Architecture and The Aphorisms of Education,* ed. H. S. Kermode. Liverpool: University of Liverpool Press, 1938.

2381 *Letters,* ed. L. P. Smith. See **2389**.

Studies

2382 ASQUITH, H. H. *Sir Henry Wotton*. London: English Association Pamphlet, #44, 1919.

2383 DATTA, K. S. "Marvell and Wotton: A Reconsideration." *RES*, 19 (1968), 403—5.

2384 HARD, F. "Sir Henry Wotton: Renaissance Englishman." *PS*, 7 (1953), 364—79.

2385 LEISHMAN, J. B. "You Meaner Beauties of the Night." *Library,* 26 (1945), 99–121.

2386 MAIN, C. F. "Wotton's 'The Character of a Happy Life.' " *Library,* 10 (1955), 270–74.

2387 MORE, P. E. "Sir Henry Wotton." *Shelburn Essays,* 5th Series. New York: Putnam's, 1908.

2388 PITMAN, M. R. "Andrew Marvell and Sir Henry Wotton." *RES,* 13 (1962), 157–58.

2389 SMITH, L. P. *The Life and Letters of Sir Henry Wotton.* New York: Oxford University Press, 1907, 1966.

2390 WALTON, I. "The Life of Sir Henry Wotton." See **2332, 2340–42.**

2391 WELD, J. S. "Some Problems of Euphuistic Narrative: Robert Greene and Wotton." *SP,* 45 (1948), 165–71.

INDEX

INDEX

INDEX

INDEX

INDEX

INDEX

INDEX

INDEX

126

INDEX

INDEX

INDEX

INDEX

INDEX

Witherspoon, A. M., 67
Witt, R. W., 1581
Wolf, A., 374
Wolf, E., II, 489
Wood, C. T., 1598
Wood, J. O., 1352
Wood, T., 2136
Wood, W. J., 2011
Woodbridge, F. J. E., 1584
Woodfield, R., 1650
Woodfill, W. L., 333
Woodhouse, A. S. P., 1017, 2209, 2312
Woodward, D. H., 1582
Worthington, E., 760
Wright, L. B., 429, 430

Wright, W. A., 519, 527
Wrigley, E. S., 536
Wykes, D., 1754
Wynter, P., 1365

Yates, F. A., 334–36
Yost, G., 656

Zeitlin, J., 620
Ziegelmaier, G., 1532
Ziegler, D. K., 703
Zitner, S. P., 1533
Zivley, S., 1158